Root & Branch

Approaches towards Understanding Tolkien

Second edition

edited by Thomas Honegger

2005

Cormarë Series

No 2

Series Editors
Peter Buchs • Thomas Honegger • Andrew Moglestue

Editor responsible for the second edition
Peter Buchs

Library of Congress Cataloging-in-Publication Data

Honegger, Thomas (ed.)
    Root and Branch. Approaches towards Understanding Tolkien.
    2nd edition.
    ISBN 3-905703-01-7

Subject headings:
Tolkien, J. R. R. (John Ronald Reuel), 1892-1973 – Criticism and interpretation
Tolkien, J. R. R. (John Ronald Reuel), 1892-1973 – Language
Fantasy fiction, English - History and criticism
Middle-earth (Imaginary place)
Literature, Comparative.

All rights reserved. No portion of this book may be reproduced, by any process or technique, without the express written consent of the publisher.

First published in 1999. 2nd Edition in 2005.
Walking Tree Publishers, Zurich and Berne 2005.
Printed by Lightning Source in the United Kingdom and the United States.

To Faolchù Fionn

Table of Contents

The Monster, the Critics, and the Public:
Literary Criticism after the Poll   1
Thomas Honegger

Section 1 – Root

The Man in the Moon: Structural Depth in Tolkien   9
Thomas Honegger

Section 2 – Branch

Tolkien and His Critics: A Critique   75
Patrick Curry

Re-enchanting Nature: Some Magic Links
between Margaret Atwood and J.R.R. Tolkien   147
Christina Ljungberg

The Monster, the Critics, and the Public: Literary Criticism after the Poll

THOMAS HONEGGER

Tolkien-bashing has been the favourite pastime of many a self-styled guardian of literary taste. The most widespread attitude towards Tolkien in institutionalised literary criticism, however, has been one of condescending ignorance and consciously cultivated neglect. It therefore came as a shock to many of those literary critics that this "horrible artifact"[1], i.e. *The Lord of the Rings*, came first not only in Waterstone's poll in 1997, but also in the two ensuing polls conducted independently by the *Daily Telegraph* and The Folio Society respectively. The 'monster' long believed dead, or at least too weak to do any harm, has taken the critics by surprise – and their panicky reactions have done nothing but to deepen the antagonism between those who do not think *The Lord of the Rings* an "horrible artifact" at all, and those who do.[2]

Most literary critics who gave more or less eloquent expression to their dismay did not go beyond superficial condemnation and the reanimation of worn prejudices.[3] The polls would have provided the ideal opportunity for a critical examination of the discrepancy between Tolkien's undisputably high public estimation and the critics' disregard for his work. Yet it was not the Tolkien-bashers who lived up to the challenge, but scholars who have been sympathetic towards Tolkien and his work. Patrick Curry's book-length study *Defending Middle-earth: Tolkien, Myth and Modernity* (1997) and

---

1 Susan Jeffreys in the *Sunday Times* on 26 January 1997 (quoted in Pearce 1998:1).
2 Pearce (1998:1-10) gives a concise overview of the critics' reactions to the polls.
3 There are flourishing Anglo-American schools of Tolkien criticism, yet only few of its proponents have their roots in traditional, institutionalised lit. crit. Numerous Tolkien scholars seem to have come to an appreciation of Tolkien via Medieval Studies or Philology – sharing thus the very sources of his inspiration.

Joseph Pearce's *Tolkien: Man and Myth* (1998) have been the first ones to provide critical discussions and possible explanations of Tolkien's continuing popular appeal[4] and the critics' dislike of his work. They were followed by Tom Shippey's *J.R.R. Tolkien: Author of the Century* (2000) and Brian Rosebury's *Tolkien: A Cultural Phenomenon* (2003), to name only the most important studies.

This controversy raging with renewed vigor in Britain seemed to have rekindled interest in Tolkien's work also in the 'neighbouring' countries, especially France and Germany. It may be due to 'chance' that the German Tolkien Society (Deutsche Tolkien Gesellschaft e.V.)[5] and the French Tolkien & Co[6] were officially founded in the same year in which the poll-results were published (1997). Furthermore, in 1998 the first two original French books on Tolkien were published.[7] Since then we have seen further publications in French, notably by Vincent Ferré (2001 and 2004) and Michaël Devaux (2003). In Germany, the Deutsche Tolkien Gesellschaft organised its first scholarly Tolkien seminar in 2004 in Cologne and the follow-up in Jena in 2005 has also been completed successfully. The publication of the first volume of *Hither Shore*, the Yearbook of the German Tolkien Society (with contributions in German and English) in 2005, was also a big step forward. It is to be hoped that the renewed interest in Tolkien in German and French speaking countries (including Switzerland) will contribute to the establishment of independent Central European schools of

---

4   Petzold (1980), who wrote the first German monograph on Tolkien, dealt with this question more than 20 years ago. A revised version (Petzold 2004) was published only recently.

5   Up to this date, it was the Inklings-Gesellschaft für Literatur und Ästhetik (Society for Literature and Aesthetics), founded in 1983 in Aachen, which devoted a considerable part of its energies to the critical discussion of Tolkien's work. Since 1983, the Inklings-Gesellschaft has published the bilingual Inklings-Jahrbuch für Literatur und Ästhetik with regular contributions on Tolkien and reviews of Tolkien-related publications.

6   La Faculté des Etudes Elfique, founded in 1987, predates Tolkien & Co by about a decade, but never adopted the necessary legal form of a 'society'. La Compagnie de la Comté was founded in 1996 and predates Tolkien & Co. by one year.

7   These are Edouard Kloczko's *Tolkien en France*, a collection of essays (with a comprehensive bibliography listing all works published on and by Tolkien in French), and Nicolas Bonnal's rather poor introductory study *Tolkien: Les Univers d'un Magicien*.

Tolkien criticism that stand in critical dialogue with the flourishing Anglo-American traditions of Tolkien-scholarship.[8]

In the introduction to the first volume of the Cormarë Series, Peter Buchs and I optimistically wrote that, in spite of Tolkien's enduring popularity, we have "been spared from the worst excesses of full-scale merchandising, in part thanks to a fairly restrictive copyright policy of the Tolkien Estate" (Buchs & Honegger 1997:1). This is, in the year one after the movies, no longer true. The movie-trilogy has succeeded in appealing to a wide public and publishers saw a sharp increase in Tolkien-readership – or at least in Tolkien-related book-sales. Yet popular success is a two-edged sword. You need some to escape oblivion, but too much of the wrong kind can cause great harm. We may have been overly optimistic in the last introduction, and I have to take a more pessimistic stance this time. Apart from the publishers who have been profiting from the movie by providing the 'book to the film', there are those who want to earn their (big) bit of money with the sale of merchandising-products related to the films – and who, since the merchandising rights to the movies have been sold together with the film-rights, cannot be controlled by the Tolkien Estate. I am looking forward to even more of those ingenious products like the ones we have been treated to so far! 'Gollum's Sushi-Knives Pack', 'Galadriel's Bathroom-Mirror', 'Longbottom Cigar Humidor' or 'Radagast Birdwatching Binoculars' – there are no limits to enterpreneurial inventiveness.

The ongoing controversy about Tolkien's literary value has inspired this second volume in the Cormarë Series – another one continuing the discussion has been published only recently (*Reconsidering Tolkien*, 2005). The contributions of this study are divided into two sections. On the one hand, we have a study that looks at Tolkien's background, sources and the influences on his work (the 'Root section', so to speak); on the other hand,

---

8   On the reception of Tolkien's work in Germany up to 1991, see Petzold (1992). See Honegger (forthcoming) for an up-to-date report.

the discussion of Tolkien's (non-)influence[9] on literature, language and society provides the common element of the 'Branch' section.

The first and, as it happens to be, only contribution in the 'Root section' looks at a structural instance of 'depth' in Tolkien's work by means of discussing the various occurrences of the Man in the Moon. The development of high and low mythologies that have grown around this character in both the real world and Middle-earth is discussed in detail and the author argues that Tolkien's multi-layered treatment of the motif imbues it with a complexity and depth that needs not shun any comparison with the real-world tradition that looks back over eight centuries.

Patrick Curry's paper heads the contributions in the 'Branch section'. His study addresses the question of why Tolkien's work is simultaneously so enduringly popular with readers and so abhorrent to literary critics. It locates the answer in what Curry defines as modernity, as a project to which the critics are heavily committed but about which the readers are very worried. Both sets of people are responding (in different ways) to the anti-modernism implicit in Tolkien's creation, which – according to the author – has been justified by subsequent events, and in the light of which his book has assumed a new and urgent set of 'postmodern' meanings. Curry criticizes Tolkien's modernist critics (including literary modernist, Marxist, feminist and psychoanalytic variants) in some detail, as well as sketching out those positive meanings.

Christina Ljungberg's study discusses parallels between Tolkien's depiction of Nature and power and the one found in Margaret Atwood's works. Although, at first sight, these two authors would seem to have little in common, a closer look reveals some intriguing affinities. Both writers use classical and popular mythologies to discuss issues of fundamental human concern; elements of the fantastic appear throughout their narratives, and both endow their characters with archetypal traits. Atwood's investigation of the metaphysical nature of *The Lord of the Rings* in her (unfinished) PhD thesis in which she fits Tolkien's work into the English tradition of the

---

9 Prof. Andreas Fischer's preliminary research with the help of the *OED* on CD-ROM has, unfortunately, not yielded sufficient data on Tolkien's assumed influence on the development of the English language (re-activation of archaic words etc.).

metaphysical romance offers interesting inroads into the works of both authors.

The original edition contained also a contribution by Andreas Bigger on the problems that would arise in the attempt to translate Tolkien's works into one of the languages spoken on the Indian subcontinent (e.g. Hindi). His article has been, upon request from the author, omitted from this new edition.

Tolkien envisioned his work as a tree to which he would add leaf after leaf. And it may be that we find these leaves so green because the roots run deeper than imagined.

References

BONNAL, Nicolas. 1998. *Tolkien: Les Univers d'un Magicien*. Paris: Les Belles Lettres.
BUCHS, Peter and Thomas HONEGGER (eds.). 1997. *News from the Shire and Beyond – Studies on Tolkien*. Second edition 2004. Zurich and Berne: Walking Tree Publishers.
CURRY, Patrick. 1997. *Defending Middle-earth: Tolkien, Myth and Modernity*. Edinburgh: Floris Books. Paperback-edition 1998 by HarperCollins.
DEVAUX, Michaël (ed.). 2003. *Tolkien, les racines du légendaire*. Geneva: Ad solem.
FERRÉ, Vincent. 2001. *Tolkien: sur les rivages de la terre du milieu*. Paris: Christian Bourgois.
FERRÉ, Vincent (ed.). 2004. *Tolkien, trente ans après (1973-2003)*. Paris: Christian Bourgois.
HONEGGER, Thomas. forthcoming. «The Reception of Tolkien's Work in Germany.» *The J.R.R. Tolkien Encyclopaedia*. New York: Routledge.
KLOCZKO, Edouard J. (ed.). 1998. *Tolkien en France*. Source Fantastique. Argenteuil: Arda.
PEARCE, Joseph. 1998. *Tolkien: Man and Myth. A Literary Life*. London: HarperCollins.
PETZOLD, Dieter. 1980. *J.R.R. Tolkien: Fantasy Literature als Wunscherfüllung und Weltdeutung*. Heidelberg: Carl Winter Universitätsverlag.
- - -. 1992. «Zwölf Jahre Tolkien-Rezeption in Deutschland, 1980-1991.» *Inklings-Jahrbuch* 10:241-255.
- - -. 2004. *Tolkien: Leben und Werk*. Eggingen: Edition Isele.
ROSEBURY, Brian. 2003. *Tolkien: A Cultural Phenomenon*. Second edition. Basingstoke: Palgrave Macmillan.
SHIPPEY, Tom . 2000. *J.R.R. Tolkien. Author of the Century*. London: HarperCollins.
TOLKIEN TIMES. Autumn 1998. London: HarperCollins.

Section 1

Root

The Man in the Moon:
Structural Depth in Tolkien

THOMAS HONEGGER

Summary

In this paper, I look at 'structural depth' in Tolkien's work by means of discussing the various occurrences of the figure of the Man in the Moon. The development of high and low mythologies that have grown around this character in both the real world and Middle-earth are investigated in detail. I argue that Tolkien's multi-layered treatment of the motif imbues it with a complexity and depth that needs not shun any comparison with the real-world tradition that looks back over eight centuries.

I Introduction: On Gleaning and Dwarves

Caxton, England's first printer, laments in his *Book of Curtesye* (c. 1478):

> Loo my child*e* / these faders auncyente // Repen the feldes fresshe of fulsomnes // The flours fresh they gadred vp & hente // [...] // Who wil it haue my childe doutles // Muste of hem begge / ther is no more to saye // [...] // Men gete it now / by cantelmele & gleyne // Here and there by besy diligence // [...] // And by the gleyne / it is ful oft sene // In whos felde / the gleyner haue bene

(Furnivall 1868:41, stanzas 58-59)

> Alas, my child, these our ancestors were able to reap the plentiful fields. The flowers (also: 'fleur de farine', i.e. the best part of the meal) they harvested and took. [...] Whoever wants (some of) this, must doubtlessly beg it from them, there is nothing else to say. [...] Men get it now by piecing together bits and by gleaning, here and

there with busy diligence. [...] And by the gleaning it can often be seen in whose field they have been.¹

Although Caxton spoke about language, poetry and eloquence, his words express a truth that transcends time and matter. As a student of Old and Middle English, I have often come across words, passages or motifs that could be assumed to have provided the sparks of inspiration for some aspects of Tolkien's sub-creation. Yet my joy of discovery has often been spoiled by realising that Tom Shippey's masterly study *The Road to Middle-earth* has already dealt with these (and many other) topics, and all that has been left for others in this field of study is to 'glean'. Yet one may look at the bright side of the situation and, changing metaphors, agree with Bernard of Chartres († 1126) that "nos esse quasi nanos gigantium humeris incidentes, ut possimus plura eis et remotiora videre, [...]" – or, in English, 'we are like dwarves sitting on the shoulders of giants, so that we are able to see more and further than they'.²

My paper gives an extensive account of the development of the Man-in-the-Moon tale in western European literature and also discusses the same motif in Tolkien's works. The Man in the Moon makes his appearance not only in Frodo's song at the 'Prancing Pony' (first published in 1923 as «The Cat and the Fiddle»), but also in a poem called «The Man in the Moon came down too soon» (first published in 1923, re-published, in a revised version, in *The Adventures of Tom Bombadil* in 1962) and in *Roverandom* (posthumously published 1998). The origin of this lunar character, however, goes back to the accounts of the creations of the sun and the moon, as to be found in *The Book of Lost Tales: Part I*.

I have endeavoured, whenever possible, to quote all the relevant poems, excerpts and passages discussed in the first part of this article in full

---

1 All translations, unless otherwise stated, are mine.
2 Ascribed to Bernard of Chartres [Bernardus Carnotensis] by John of Salisbury [Joannes Saresberiensis, 1120-1180] in the fourth chapter of the third book of his *Metalogicus* (c. 1159; to be found in vol. 199 [0900 C] of the *Patrologiae Latinae*, ed. J.P. Migne, Paris 1853, re-published on CD ROM by Chadwyck-Healey Inc. 1995).
Merton (1965) gives a highly entertaining as well as eminently learned account of the reception of this metaphor throughout the centuries.

and in the original languages (with an accompanying translation). The disadvantage of this practice is, of course, that the paper grew in length but not necessarily in substance. Yet, I considered the advantage of providing all the relevant data from the original sources to outweigh any disadvantages incurred, not least since many of the works quoted are not that easily accessible. Grosart's edition of Dekker, for example, has been printed in 50 copies for private circulation only and I do not expect my readers to have volume III at hand to check a reference like "Dek. III, pp.171ff., Gros.", as I had the pleasure to do. In addition to this, some of the previous overview articles on the topic of the Man in the Moon give either outdated, incomplete or even incorrect bibliographical references – something I have remedied as far as possible. And last, but not least, some new references to passages not yet mentioned have been added to the list.

II The Man in the Moon

I will first give an overview of the occurrences of the Man in the Moon in European literature and discuss possible origin(s) and meaning(s) and, subsequently, present the treatment of the motif in Tolkien's work. The complexity of the matter makes it necessary to delineate the development of this figure in detail, especially since we find a similar complex development of the Man in the Moon in Tolkien's universe. However, I have tried and restricted myself to present only those facts that are either of relevance for the understanding of the argument or that provide insight into the nature of the Man in the Moon in Tolkien's work. All other information has been relegated to the appendices.

1 Survivals into (early) modern times and their sources

The Man in the Moon, whose outline may be discerned in the full moon as seen from the northern hemisphere, is a familiar figure. Most speakers of English make his acquaintance at a relatively early age since he is the protagonist of one of the traditional nursery rhymes:

No. 331

The man in the moon
Came down too soon,
And asked his way to Norwich;
He went by the south,
And burnt his mouth
With supping cold plum porridge.
(Opie 1997:346)

Illustration by Leslie Brooke (1913)
The Man in the Moon / Came tumbling down

Illustration by Leslie Brooke (1913)
And ask'd his way to Norwich

Illustration by Leslie Brooke (1913)
They told him south, / And he burnt his mouth / With eating cold pease-porridge.

A variant of this nursery rhyme is given in Halliwell (1970:221). It avoids the paradox of 'burning one's mouth with cold porridge' and changes the passage to "And burnt his mouth / With supping hot pease-porridge." This version makes more sense (if 'sense' is a relevant criterion in nursery rhymes) and may prove useful to teach some table manners to children – parental advice such as 'Don't gobble down your hot porridge, or you will burn your mouth like the Man in the Moon!' would be somewhat difficult with the 'cold plum porridge' version.

The Man in the Moon also features in several ballads and songs, from which we learn even more about his culinary predilections:

No. 332a

The man in the moon drinks claret,
But he is a dull jack-a-dandy;
Would he know a sheep's head from a carrot
He should learn to drink cider and brandy.
(Opie 1997:348)

Illustration from Harley (1885:12)
The Man in the Moon drinks claret.

Iona and Peter Opie (1997:348) note that it is said to be "the first stanza of a traditional Somersetshire song. It appears to be stemmed from, or part quoted in, a ballad in *Le Prince d'Amour* (1660). This was reprinted about 1673 on a broadside, and again two years later (registered 1 Mar. 1675) when it was titled: *New Mad Tom of Bedlam* [...]." The ballad ends:

No. 332b

The man in the Moon drinks Clarret;
With Powder-beef, Turnep and Carret,[3]
A Cup of old Malago Sack
Will fire his bush at his back.
(Opie 1997:348)

While one may accept the Man in the Moon's rather peculiar selection of drink and food as part of the fun and rhyme, the 'bush at his back' raises some questions. Things get even more mysterious in yet another rhyme:

No. 333

The Man in the Moon was caught in a trap
For stealing the thorns from another man's gap.
If he had gone by, and let the thorns lie,
He'd never been Man in the Moon so high.
(Opie 1997:349)

Iona and Peter Opie (1997:349) add the following comment to No. 333:

> This rhyme, heard by a contributor to *Folk-Lore* (1913), gives the traditional picture of the Man in the Moon who is identified by his lantern and bush of thorns (as in *A Midsummer Night's Dream*). The legend is that the man was banished to the moon for strewing a church path with thorns to hinder the people attending mass.

---

3   'Powder-beef' is salted beef, 'carret' is a variant of 'carat', the seed or bean of the carob-tree.

Although foreshortening, mixing and thus distorting some of the different traditions attached to the figure of the Man in the Moon, the commentary establishes some of the basic facts of the wider, and probably less nonsensical picture that has been only briefly glimpsed in the nursery rhymes and ballads. Thus, the '[thorn] bush at his back' (in No. 332b) is obviously to be identified with the 'thorns' mentioned in rhyme No. 333. In order to explain and clarify the (in this form faulty and misleading) reference to the legend of the thorn-strewing man, it is necessary to go back in time and review the existing evidence.

A Thorny Burden

The earliest known English writer to mention the Man in the Moon with his thorny burden is Alexander Neckam (1157-1217). Chapter XIV of the first book of his treatise *De Naturis Rerum* is headed «De macula lunae» ('About the mark/blemish of the moon'). Neckam discusses the various theories concerning the origin and nature of the 'shadow' or 'mark' on the moon – theories that recur time and again in connection with speculations on the nature of the moon throughout the centuries.[4] Some say, he reports, that the surface of the moon is riddled with caves that do not admit sunlight and thus cause areas of shadow. Others say that the moon is not a smooth globe, but that it has parts that protrude and others that are concave and are therefore not reached by the sunlight. A third group believes that the material the moon is made of is not of a consistently fair texture, and that the shadowy parts are simply areas of darker matter. He then continues:

> Sed sciendum est, in signum et in instructionem nostri factum esse. Merito enim praevaricationis primorum parentum, omnium planetarum et stellarum fulgor dispendium claritatis sustinuit. Luna vero, quae citima terris est, et aspectibus humanis familiarius occurrens, maculam in se retinuit, ad denotandum quod quamdiu in statu vitae praesentis currimus, macula aliqua in sancta ecclesia est. [...] Forsitan simplex lector non advertit quid vocem lunae maculam. Nonne novisti

---

4   Nicolson (1936) discusses these aspects in her study on the changing attitude towards the moon in early modern times.

quid vulgus vocet rusticum in luna portantem spinas? Unde quidam vulgariter loquens, ait:
>Rusticus in luna, quem sarcina deprimit una
>Monstrat per spinas nulli prodesse rapinas.

Quotiens igitur umbram illam dispersam conspicis, revoca ad memoriam transgressionem primorum parentum, et ingemisce.
(Wright 1863:53-54)

But it must be known that this [i.e. the mark] is made as a sign and for our instruction. As a consequence of the misdeed of the first parents [i.e. Adam and Eve], all planets and stars have endured a loss of splendour. The moon, however, being closest to the earth, and a familiar view to humans, retained a proper mark (or: blemish) so as to signify that while we are in the state of the present life, there is also a blemish in the Holy Church. [...] It may be that the simple reader has not noticed what I call 'the mark of the moon'. Don't you know that which the common crowd calls 'The peasant in the moon, who carries thorns'? Therefore one says commonly:
>The peasant in the moon, whom a (certain) bundle weighs down
>Illustrates through the thorns that stealing is never profitable

Thus, whenever you perceive its scattered shadow, remember the transgression of the forefathers [i.e. Adam and Eve] and groan over it.

Thus, Alexander Neckam interprets the mark of the moon as a direct consequence and reminder of the biblical Fall of Man. He mentions the figure of the 'thorn-carrying rustic' in an aside and only to ensure that it becomes clear what is meant with 'macula lunae'. This 'rusticus in luna', then, is the subject of a Middle English poem from the early 14th century, handed down in Harley Manuscript no. 2253. Since it lacks a title, like most medieval literary texts, it is usually referred to as «The Man in the Moon». The edition used is Bennet and Smithers' (1974:127-28):

>Mon in þe mone stond and strit;
>The Man in the moon stands and strides
>On is bot-forke is burþen he bereþ.
>On his hay-fork his burden he bears.
>Hit is muche wonder þat he n'adoun slyt–
>It is a great wonder that he does not slip down–
>For doute leste he valle he shoddreþ ant shereþ!
>For fear of falling he shudders and swerves!
>When þe forst feseþ, muche chele he byd.   5
>When the frost freezes, great cold he suffers.

þe þornes beþ kene–is hattren totereþ.
The thorns are sharp–his clothes [they] tear.
Nis no wyþt in þe world þat wont wen he syt,
There is no wight [person?] in the world that knows when he sits down,
Ne (bote hit bue þe hegge) whet wedes he wereþ.
Nor (unless it is the hedgerow) what clothes he wears.

Whider troweþ þis mon ha þe wey take?
Where do you think this man has taken the way [i.e. where does he go]?
He haþ set is o fot oþer toforen.   10
He has set his one foot in front of his other.
For non hiþte þat he haþ ne syþt me hym ner shake–
For no haste he has nor does one see him ever at all move–
He is þe sloweste mon þat euer wes yboren.
He is the slowest man that ever was born.
Wher he were o þe feld pycchynde stake,
Wherever he might be in the field driving stakes,
For hope of ys þornes to dutten is doren,
In hope of his thorns for closing his gaps,
He mot myd is twybyl oþer trous make,   15
He must, with his two-edged axe, other cuttings [of thorn] make,
Oþer al is dayes werk þer were yloren.
Or else all his day's work there would be lost.

þis ilke mon vpon heh when er he were,
This same man upon high whenever he was,
Wher he were y þe mone boren ant yfed,
Where [whether?] he had been in[to] the moon taken and sustained [fed],
He leneþ on is forke ase a grey frere.
He leans on his fork as a gray friar [i.e. Franciscan].
þis crokede caynard sore he is adred!   20
This bent idler, very much is he afraid!
Hit is mony day go þat he was here.
It is many a day ago that he was here.
Ichot of is ernde he haþ nout ysped:
I know of his business, he has not succeeded at all:
He haþ hewe sumwher a burþen of brere–
He has cut down somewhere a bundle of briar
þarefore sum hayward haþ taken ys wed.
for this some hedge-keeper has taken a security
[i.e. a pledge for payment of a fine] from him.

'3ef þy wed ys ytake, bring hom þe trous! 25
'If your pledge is taken, bring home the bundle!
Sete forþ þyn oþer fot, stryd ouer sty!
Set forth your other foot, stride over the path!
We shule preye þe haywart hom to vr hous
We shall ask the hedge-keeper home to our house
Ant maken hym at heyse for þe maystry–
And make him at ease in the highest degree–
Drynke to hym deorly of fol god bous,
Give him to drink heartily of very good liquor ['booze']
Ant oure dame Douse shal sitten hym by. 30
And our lady Douse [or: sweet lady] will sit next to him.
When þat he is dronke ase a dreynt mous,
When that he is as drunk as a drowned mouse,
þenne we schule borewe þe wed ate bayly.'
Then we will redeem the pledge at [from?] the bailiff.'

þis mon hereþ me nout, þah Ich to hym crye;
This man hears me not, though I shout to him;
Ichot þe cherl is def – þe del hym todrawe!
I know, the churl is deaf –the devil tear him to pieces!
þah Ich 3e3e vpon heþ nulle nout hye– 35
Though I cry aloud, he does not want to hurry at all–
þe lostlase ladde con nout o lawe.
The surly fellow cannot [come] down [or: knows nothing about the law]
Hupe forþ, Hubert, hosede pye!
Hop forth, Hubert, you hosed magpie!
Ichot þart amarscled into þe mawe.
I know you are bewildered [or: enchanted] to your very vitals.
or: I know you are stained into your maw [cf. the bird's varying black & white colouring]
þah me teone wiþ hym þat myn teh mye,
Though I am vexed with him so that my teeth grate,
þe cherld nul nout adoun er þe day dawe. 40
The churl does not want [to come] down before the day dawns.

Although there are still some lines that remain disputed or whose meaning is simply not clear to anyone, scholarly research into medieval hedge-planting and its legal implications (cf. Menner 1949) has provided vital information to the understanding of at least the most important allusions and references. Thus it was part of each villager's duty to either build or repair already existing hedges on his strip of land in order to protect the fields from stray sheep and cattle that would damage the crops. Lines 5-8 of the Middle English poem refer obviously to the business of repairing a hedge by driving stakes (that will keep the protective bundles of thorns in place) and planting the live slips of cuttings of plants. The quick-sets must be protected from being eaten or trampled on by cattle or sheep until they have grown. This is done by covering them with thorns. It is thus the newly-planted live slips, the Man in the Moon's 'dayes werk', that are in danger unless they are protected by additional bundles of thorns, which he seems to have gathered without the permission of the landlord (line 23). The hedge-warden, who is in charge of overseeing the planting and keeping in repair of the hedges in his district, must have caught him red handed and, since the Man in the Moon possessed no money to pay the fine for his trespass, he had to give a pledge of security (line 24; the nature of the 'wed' (< lat. 'vadium'), i.e. pledge, is not mentioned, but it could be something like his axe or his cloak). This pledge could then be redeemed by paying the fine.

An English seal from the first half of the fourteenth century shows our Man in the Moon, accompanied by a dog, carrying what may be identified as a thorn-bush. It is the seal of Walter de Grendon (c. 1320-35) and the inscription around the seal reads: TE WALTER DOCEBO CVR SPINAS PHEBO GERO, which may be translated as 'I will teach thee, Walter, why I carry thorns in the moon.' The teaching part, if there has ever been one, is unfortunately lost and the inscription remains rather enigmatic. The picture reproduced underneath is taken from Heslop (1987:116), the drawing from Baring-Gould (1906:198)[5]:

---

5 The drawing and a discussion of the seal are allegedly to be found in *The Archæological Journal* (March 1848:66-67). I did not have the opportunity to check this reference.

Reginald Pecock (c.1395-1460), in chapter IV of the second part of his *The Repressor of Over Much Blaming of the Clergy* (c. 1449), mentions the popular belief in the Man in the Moon as a harmless superstition (in contrast to morally vicious ones):

> Sum other vntrewe opinioun of men is such that for it her conuersacioun schal not be maad the worse moralli, or ellis not a3ens notable, good, vertuose moralte; as is this opinioun, that a man which stale sumtyme a birthan of thornis was sett in to the moone, there forto abide for euere;
>
> (Babington 1860, volume 1:155)

> Another superstition of men is of such nature that for it their manner of living will not be made the worse morally, or else [it is] not against notable, good virtuous morality; as is the belief that a man who once stole a burden of thorns was set into the moon, there to remain forever.

Half a century or so later, we find another literary reference to the 'lunatic thorn-thief' in the *Testament of Cresseid* by the Scottish poet Robert Henryson (c.1430-c.1506). He writes of Lady Cynthia, i.e. the moon:

> Hir gy[t]e was gray and full of spottis blak,
> Her mantle was gray and full of black spots,
> And on hir breist ane churle paintit full euin
> And on her breast was depicted very precisely a churl

> Beirand ane bunche of thornis on his bak,
> carrying a bundle of thorns on his back,
> Quhilk for his thift micht clim na nar the heuin.
> Who for his theft may climb no nearer up to heaven.
> (Fox 1968:70, ll. 260-63)

This is, to my knowledge, the only example where the Man in the Moon occurs side by side (or rather: back to breast) with a traditional allegorical representation of the Moon as a woman; a tradition that goes back to the moon goddess of antiquity.[6]

All references to the Man in the Moon so far, i.e. the ones by Neckam, the anonymous author of the Middle English poem, Pecock, and Henryson, identify him as a thorn-thief – as is the protagonist of the nursery rhyme No. 333. Stealing thorns, then, is something that makes sense in the context of medieval English hedge-making. Yet if it is transferred to another place or time, it may lose its original meaning and puzzle the audience;[7] it is very probable that another explanation will be sought – and invariably found. Baring-Gould (1906:193) mentions stories from Schaumburg-Lippe, Swabia and Marken. They place a man and a woman in the moon. The man stands there because he strewed brambles and thorns on the church path, in order to hinder people from attending Mass on Sunday morning;[8] the woman because she made butter on Sunday, the day of the Lord on which all work has to cease. As a sign of their trespasses, the man carries his bundle of thorns on his back, the woman her butter-tub. Iona and Peter Opie's 'explanation' of No. 333 is therefore an attempt to make sense of the enigmatic and, as it stands for modern readers, rather pointless thorn-theft by placing it within the context of the 'thorns on the path to Mass' incident. Yet since No. 333 contains no reference to such an incident at all, it seems more appropriate to interpret it as a later companion-piece to the Middle

---

6   Works that make use of the classical tradition are Michael Drayton's *Endimion & Phoebe* (1606; ed. Hebel 1931, volume 1:125-156) and Lyly's *Endymion* (1588; ed. Bevington 1996).

7   Gittée (1901:397), for example, thinks that stealing thorns or wood is too trivial a crime to account for the punishment of the Man in the Moon.

8   Grimm (1883:717, fn. 2) refers to a Westphalian story about a man who dressed the church with thorns on Sunday, and was therefore put, bundle and all, onto the moon.

English poem and to view the thorn-theft within the context of medieval hedge-growing.

2 Quid enim Cain cum spinis - What has Cain to do with thorns?

The English (and Scottish) writers discussed in the preceding chapters are not the only authors who refer to the Man in the Moon and his burden. Outside Britain, the earliest known reference to the Man in the Moon is found in Dante (1265-1321). In Canto XX of his *Inferno*, he writes:

> Ma vienne omai, ché già tiene 'l confine
> d'amendue li emisperi e tocca l'onda
> sotto Sobilia Caino e le spine;
> e già iernotte fu la luna tonda:
> ben ten de' ricordar, ché non ti nocque
> alcuna volta per la selva fonda.
>
> But now come, for already Cain with his thorns holds the confines of both hemispheres [i.e. the hemisphere that has Jerusalem at its centre and the hemisphere of water], and touches the wave below Seville [i.e. in setting in the West, as seen by an observer ideally stationed in Jerusalem]: and already last night the moon was round. You must remember it well, for it did you no harm sometimes in the deep wood.
> (Text and translation from Singleton 1970:210-211, ll. 124-129)

Here, 'Cain with his thorns' stands for the moon itself. Another reference to Cain as the Man in the Moon occurs in Canto II of *Paradiso*:

> Ma ditemi: che son li segni bui
> di questo corpo, che là giuso in terra
> fan di Cain favoleggiare altrui?
>
> But tell me, what are the dusky marks of this body which there below on earth cause folk to tell the tale of Cain?
> (Text and translation from Singleton 1975:16-18, lines 49-51)

Singleton (1970, Part 2:362) comments: "According to the Italian tradition, Cain attempted to excuse himself for the murder of Abel and was condemned by God to be confined to the moon." This is all very well, but it does not explain the thorns and one may be tempted to ask with Alcuin[9] 'Quid enim Cain cum spinis?' – 'What has Cain to do with thorns?'. In order to see further in this matter and to find a tentative answer, we have to climb onto someone else's shoulders.

Emerson (1906b), in his nearly book-length article on the legends of Cain in Old and Middle English, believes that the story about Cain's banishment to the moon has been known in Britain, too. Yet Neckam, whose interpretation of the mark on the moon as the result of Adam and Eve's transgression would have provided the ideal opportunity to mention any Cain-legends, remains silent on this matter. Thus, we have to wait for quite a while until we come across any evidence that illuminates the connection between Cain and thorns, and thus with the thorn-carrying Man in the Moon. The Cornish mystery *Gwreans an Bys: The Creation of the World* (c. 1611, attributed to William Jordan) presents Cain as a farmer who refuses to sacrifice from the first fruits of the field to God, but instead burns thorns and weeds and dung on the altar (this elaboration is not to be found in the original account in *Genesis*):

> [Cain to Abel]
> ye lysky ny vannaf ve
> Burn it I will not
> an eys nan frutes defrye
> The corn nor the fruits certainly:
> > taw abell thymo pedn cowge
> > Be silent, Abel, to me, dolt-head!
>
> me a guntell dreyne ha spearn
> I will gather brambles and thorns
> ha glose tha leskye heb bearn
> And dry cowdung to burn without regret,
> > hag a ra bush brase a vooge
> > And will make a great bush of smoke.
>
> (edited and translated by Stokes 1863:88-89, ll. 1088-1093)

---

9 Alcuin, in a letter to bishop Speratus of Lindisfarne in A.D. 797, reproaches the monks for listening to secular tales and songs about (pagan) Germanic heroes ('carmina gentilium') instead of readings from the Scriptures or the Fathers ('sermones patrum') and asks provocatively: 'Quid enim Hinieldus cum Christo?' – 'What has Ingeld [a Germanic hero] to do with Christ?'

A similar reluctant Cain is presented in the *Mactatio Abel* (Cawley 1958:1-13) of the Wakefield pageants in the Towneley Cycle (c. 1400-1450), though there the thorns (mentioned in line 202f.) are not explicitly referred to as part of the offering.

The only unambiguous connection between Cain and the Man in the Moon in an English text has been reported by Paget Toynbee (1906:776) in a letter to *The Athenæum*. He quotes from "a rare seventeenth-century booklet, entitled *The Strange Fortune of Alerane; or, My Ladies Toy* (London, 1605)"[10] the following passage:

> [The author is speaking of two hapless lovers the course of whose true love was not running smooth: –]
>
> But see how Cupid like a cruell (Caine)
> Doth change faire daies and makes it frowning weather:
> These Princes joyes, he over cast with paine,
> For 'twas not likely they should match together.

However, whether the unnamed author of *The Strange Fortune or Alerane; or, My Ladies Toy* makes his reference in view of an alleged ancient English tradition that identifies Cain with the Man in the Moon, or whether he has just read his Dante, remains a moot point.

Yet Emerson (1906b:840-845), in spite of the scanty evidence and its often merely circumstantial nature, believes that this tradition has been known in England and quotes the lines with which King Henry (Bolingbroke) banishes the murderer of King Richard in Shakespeare's *Richard II*:

> With Cain go wander through the shades of night,
> And never show thy head by day nor light.
> (*Richard II* 5.6.43-44; Greenblatt 1997:1012)

He assumes that 'wander through the shades of night' refers to the 'Cain in the moon' tradition. Yet, in my opinion, it may equally well be a poetic elaboration of the biblical account of Cain's wanderings after his banishment by God.

---

10 It must be a rare booklet indeed since I have not been able to find either the booklet itself or any additional reference to it.

The chain of reasoning proposed by Emerson runs like this: First, the English tradition has a Man in the Moon who carries a burden of thorns (Neckam et al.). Second, the Italian tradition (Dante) identifies this thorn-carrying figure with Cain. Third, Cain is associated with thorns (*Gwreans an Bys: The Creation of the World*) and with the moon (*Richard II* and *The Strange Fortune of Alerane; or, My Ladies Toy*) in Britain, too. From this follows that the British thorn-carrying Man in the Moon has to be identified with Cain. q.e.d.

I leave it to the reader to weigh the evidence and to judge the soundness of this hypothesis.

The Italian tradition of identifiying the Man in the Moon with Cain, whether known in medieval Britain or not, is important in another aspect. The Man in the Moon is no longer an anonymous and slightly comic figure, but becomes an identifiable personage from biblical mythology.

3 In a company of thieves and knaves

The 'Italian' Cain's banishment to the moon as punishment for the fratricide connects him with the tradition of the Man in the Moon as transgressor against divine law who then suffers the same penalty. A popular legend identifies the Man in the Moon with the Sabbath-breaker of *Numbers* xv.32-36. He is caught gathering sticks on the Sabbath day and is brought before Moses and Aaron to be judged. God orders Moses to put him to death and the culprit is stoned. Several European legends seem to have taken their inspiration from this incident, though the Sabbath-breaker (usually gathering firewood on a Sunday) is no longer stoned but banished into the moon (as was the butter-churning woman mentioned above). There are a few medieval depictions of such a figure of a Man in the Moon carrying a bundle of sticks, often accompanied by a dog.[11] Thus, Baring-Gould (1906: 197-98) points to an 'ancient' pictorial representation of a Man in the Moon

---

11 Emerson (1906b:844) writes that, "according to one tradition, a dog was given him [i.e. Cain] to lead him in his wanderings" and interprets the appearance of a dog as additional evidence for his theory.

carrying a bundle of sticks in Gyffyn Church near Conway (cf. drawing, from Baring-Gould 1906:198; the same drawing appears in Harley 1885:32, who is likely to have it from Baring-Gould's earlier edition (1866) of *Curious Myths of the Middle Ages*):

Representation in Gyffyn Church, near Conway

It is this bundle-carrying, lantern-holding and dog-owning Man in the Moon who is depicted 'asking his way to Norwich' in Andrew Lang's *The Nursery Rhyme Book*, which Tolkien is likely to have known, and again in the anonymous *The Man in the Moon: A Nursery Rhyme Picture Book* (1913).

L. Leslie Brooke's illustration to the nursery-rhyme "The man in the moon, / Came tumbling down, / And ask'd his way to Norwich, / He went by the south, / And burnt his mouth / With supping cold pease-porridge." (Lang 1897:55)

There are several other, related stories about the Man in the Moon (see Grimm 1883, Baring-Gould 1906:190-203, Harley 1885:5-53 and Gittée 1901). In the great majority of those he is exiled to the moon because he has been caught stealing something (thorns, wood, willow bows, cabbages, sheep etc.), or because he has transgressed against the commandments of religion (breaking the Sabbath, keeping others from attending Mass, dressing the church with thorns on Sunday). He either remains anonymous or, as in the Middle English poem, he has a name like 'Hubert', which, however, provides no further clue to his identity.[12]

Yet not only biblical mythology provides a name for our friend in the moon. Snorri Sturluson (1179-1241), in his *(Prose or Younger) Edda*, a work well known to Tolkien, relates the following story in the «Gylfaginning»:

> Hárr segir: 'Sá maðr er nefndr Mundilfari, er átti tvau börn. Þau váru svá fögr ok fríð, at hann kallði son sinn Mána, en dóttur sína Sól ok gifti hana þeim manni, er Glenr hét. En goðin reiddust þessu ofdrambi ok tóku þau systkin ok settu upp á himin, létu Sól keyra þá hesta, er drógu kerru sólarinnar, þeirar er goðin höfðu skapat til at lysa heimana af þeiri síu, er flaug ór Muspellsheimi. Þeir hestar heita svá, Árvakr ok Alsviðr, en undir bógum hestanna settu goðin tvá vindbelgi at kæla þá, en í sumum fræðum er þat kallat ísarnkol. Máni styrir göngu tungls ok ræðr nyjum ok niðum. Hann tók tvau börn af jörðunni, er svá heita, Bil ok Hjúki, er þau gengu frá brunni þeim, er Byrgir heitir, ok báru á öxlum sér sá, er heitir Sægr, en stöngin Simul. Viðfinnr er nefndr faðir þeira. Þessi börn fylgja Mána, svá sem sjá má af jörðu.
>
> (Jónsson 1954:21-22)

> High said: 'There was a person whose name was Mundilfaeri who had two children. They were so fair and beautiful that he called the one Moon [Mâni] and his daughter Sol, and gave her in marriage to a person called Glen. But the gods got angry at this arrogance and took the brother and sister and set them up in the sky; they made Sol drive the horses that drew the chariot of the sun which the gods had created, to illuminate the worlds, out of the molten particle that had flown out of the world of Muspell. The names of these horses are Arvak and Alsvinn. Under the shoulders of these horses the gods put two bellows to cool them, and in some sources it is called ironblast. Moon [Mâni] guides the course of the moon and controls its waxing and waning. He took two children from the earth called Bil and Hiuki as they were leaving a well called Byrgir, carrying between them on their shoulders a tub called Saeg; their carrying-pole was called Simul. Their father's name was Vidfinn. These children go with Moon, as can be seen from earth.'
>
> (Faulkes 1987:14)

---

12 On the possible connection between Chaucer's Friar Huberd in *The Canterbury Tales* and the Man in the Moon, see Reiss (1963).

Grimm (1883:717) remarks that this tradition seems to have survived into modern times since Swedish people see in the spots of the moon two persons carrying a big bucket on a pole. Grimm (1883:717) and Gittée (1901:387) believe the person-abducting, heathen moon god Mâni to be the prototype of the (Christian) 'thieving Man in the Moon'. The theft as the central element, so they argue, has been retained, while all other elements underwent far-reaching changes. Thus, Gittée (1901:395) identifies the 'chanson de geste' hero Basin as one of the forms under which Mâni continues his existence. This Basin, a master-thief and opponent of Charlemagne, is the main protagonist in *Jehan de Lanson* and occurs also in other texts that centre around Charlemagne.

4 Later developments

The medieval tradition transformed

Almost all later, and also some earlier depictions of the figure in the moon omit any references to the thorn-theft. Authors either mention the Man in the Moon only briefly, as does Chaucer (1340-1400) in *Troilus and Criseyde* (I 1023-24),[13] or they present him as the probably by now 'traditional' figure with a thornbush, and sometimes a dog and a lantern, but without attempting to provide an explanation for these attributes. Shakespeare (1564–1616) and his contemporaries depict him in his traditional form, and the Man in the Moon makes his most famous appearance in Shakespeare's *A Midsummer Night's Dream*:[14]

> *Quince*: Ay, or else one must come in with a bush of thorns and a lantern and say he comes to disfigure, or to present, the person of Moonshine.

(*A Midsummer Night's Dream* 3.1.51-53; Greenblatt 1997:832)

---

[13] Pandarus chides Troilus: "Thow hast ful gret care / Lest that the cherl may falle out of the moone!" This can be translated as 'You worry even about the possibility that the churl [the Man in the Moon] may fall out of the moon!', which means that Pandarus thinks that Troilus worries too much.

[14] For additional examples of the medieval tradition transformed, see Appendix I.

> *Starveling* [as Moon]: All that I have to say is to tell you that the lantern is the moon, I the man i'th' moon, this thorn bush my thorn bush, and this dog my dog.

(*A Midsummer Night's Dream* 5.1.247-249; Greenblatt 1997:856)

From the seventeenth century onwards, the Man in the Moon is no longer a solitary resident on the moon, but shares his abode with others. This new development finds its most famous and influential proponent in (Bishop) Francis Godwin's (1562-1633) travel-account *The Man in the Moone* (first published 1638; cf. Butler 1995).[15] His work is the first travel account of a journey to the moon since Lucian of Samosata's *Icaromenippus*. Godwin's narrator, Domingo Gonzalez, flies to the moon by means of an 'engine' drawn by geese ('gansas'). It takes him twelve days to get there, which is far longer than it took Rover on the back of the seagull in Tolkien's *Roverandom* (Tolkien 1998:19-22) – and yet the description of Gonzalez's flight is worth quoting since it bears some resemblance to the one in Tolkien's children-story:

> For I cannot imagine that a bullet out of the mouth of a cannon could make way through the vaporous and muddy air near the earth with that celerity, which is most strange, considering that my gansas moved their wings but now and then, and sometimes not at all in a quarter of an hour together, only they held them stretched out, so passing on as we see the eagles and kites will do for a little space, [...]

(Butler 1995:92)

Gonzalez approaches the moon and observes

> that it was covered for the most part with a huge and mighty sea, whose parts only being dry land which show unto us here somewhat darker than the rest of her body, that I mean which the country people call *el hombre de la luna*, the man of the moon.

(Butler 1995:93)

---

15 Nicolson (1960) gives a comprehensive overview on stories about voyages to the moon.

Thus, the 'popular' interpretation of the mark on the moon is contrasted with the 'correct' one as a landscape feature. Gonzalez's sojourn on the moon gives him the opportunity to learn some of the language and custom of the oversized inhabitants[16], the Lunars, and tells us, among many other things, how they get rid of their potential criminals:

> And because it is an inviolable decree amongst them never to put anyone to death, perceiving by the stature and some other notes they have who are likely to be of a wicked or imperfect disposition, they send them away (I know not by what means) into the earth, and change them for other children before they shall have either ability or opportunity to do amiss amongst them. [...] And their ordinary vent for them is a certain high hill in the north of America, whose people I can easily believe to be wholly descended of them, [...]. Sometimes they mistake their aim, and fall upon Christendom, Asia, or Africa; marry, that is but seldom.
> (Butler 1995:106-107)

This throws a rather different light on why the Man in the Moon came tumbling down.

Godwin's overall presentation of the realm of the Lunars is in many ways indebted to the utopian tradition. The fact that he had chosen the moon as the 'Blessed Realm' may point to a link with the Hellenistic tradition which held that the blessed souls inhabited the moon. Butler, in his introduction to *The Man in the Moone*, comments: "It was natural, then, for a traveller setting out to look for a better world to go to the Moon" (Butler 1995:21). This is especially true in a time when the great discoveries seem to have left little space for utopian empires within the limits of this earth.[17]

---

16 In the wake of Galileo's *Sidereus nuncius* (1610; cf. the edition by van Helden 1989), in which he describes the observations he made with his telescope, especially about the nature of the lunar surface, several influential scholars (Tomaso Campanella, Thomas Digges, Johannes Kepler, and Giordano Bruno) expressed their belief in the possiblity that the moon might be inhabited.

17 For the occurrence of the Man in the Moon in social and political satires, in scientific works, and in idiomatic and proverbial expressions, see Appendices II and III.

The classical tradition transformed

Although the moon goddess Cynthia has been mentioned in connection with the thorn-stealing Man in the Moon by Henryson, the two traditions usually do not mix. The Man in the Moon and the Moon remain two distinct entities, even though they may occur side by side. Lyly, in his *Endymion* (1588), refers several times to the Man in the Moon and actually calls his play *Endymion, The Man in the Moon*. He implicitly identifies Endymion with the Man in the Moon in the prologue: "Most high and happy princess, we must tell you a tale of the Man in the Moon, which, if it seem ridiculous for the method, or superfluous for the matter, or for the means incredible, for three faults we can make but one excuse: it is a tale of the Man in the Moon." (Bevington 1996:78). However, when Endymion is introduced as a lovesick youth, we find the following exchange between him and his friend Eumenides:

> *Eumenides*: I hope you be not sotted upon the man in the moon.
> *Endymion*: No, but settled either to die or possess the moon herself.
>
> (Bevington 1996:80, I.1.16-19)

The Man in the Moon occurs once more in the song of the watch:

> *Watch*: Stand. Who goes there?
> We charge you appear
> 'Fore our constable here.
> In the name of the Man in the Moon,
> To us billmen relate
> Why you stagger so late,
> And how you come drunk so soon.
>
> (Bevington 1996:152-153, IV.2.127-133)

Things are obviously not that clear – with Endymion still walking the earth, how can he be at the same time the Man in the Moon? And why do the watchmen derive their authority from him? But such minor inconsistencies are easily overlooked by both audience and author since the classical myth of Endymion and the moon goddess Cynthia and the popular belief in the Man in the Moon exist on two parallel yet separated levels.

The 'separation' of classical myth and popular tradition can be observed in the way the moon is depicted. On the one hand, we have pictorial works that focus on the Man in the Moon (cf. the depictions on pp.12-14, 21 and 27-28). On the other hand, the classical tradition of personifying the Sun and Moon is still alive. Thus, in "medieval examples the sun and moon may be represented in their classical forms: the sun as a male figure driving a 'quadriga', the moon as a female driving a team of oxen, each within a circular disk." (Hall 1974:86).[18] The tradition to depict the Sun as a face within a flaming disk and the Moon as a female face that makes up the full circle of the crescent of the moon becomes increasingly popular from the thirteenth century onward (cf. picture below). Thus, the moon god(dess) often occurs as a personification of the planet, while the Man in the Moon is merely associated with the moon,[19] and I doubt whether Lady Cynthia has ever been involved in thorn-stealing.

Moon from the ceiling of the 'Alten Rathaus' (Old City Hall) Munich by Erasmus Gasser (15th century) (Müller-Meiningen 1984:69)

---

18 The idea of a 'moon-chariot' occurs also in Drayton's *Endimion and Phoebe* (1606) where Phoebe approaches "Mounted aloft upon her Cristall Coach, / Drawn or'e the playnes by foure pure milk-white Hinds" (Hebel 1931, volume 1:150, lines 830-831).

19 The Man in the Moon, as part of the moon, may be used metonymically for the moon itself. Yet he does not attain the same status as his pagan counterpart, the goddess of the moon.

5 The Man in the Moon rediscovered

The folk-belief in the Man in the Moon, as we have seen, was only faintly remembered in idiomatic expressions (cf. Appendix III, p. 63) and in increasingly puzzling fragments of nursery rhymes. As an independent motif, it had more or less disappeared from literature. Thus, in the nineteenth century, the time had come to 're-discover' this motif. On the one hand, we find lyrical poems on the Man in the Moon, while on the other, children's books developed the motif in their own way.

Poetry

An anonymous poet who identifies himself as 'an Undergraduate of Worcester College, London, and of the Inner Temple, London',[20] published a poem with the very original and rare title *The Man in the Moon* (in two parts 1839 [540 lines] and 1840 [442 lines]) several decades before Tolkien penned the first version of his Man-in-the-Moon poems. I will provide the entire first stanza and parts of the later ones, as well as a brief summary. I do so since this poem provides several parallels to Tolkien's *The Man in the Moon Came Down Too Soon*.

> *The Man in the Moon.*
> (1839, by an Undergraduate of Worcester College, London)
>
> I
>
> The Man in the Moon! why came he down
> From his peaceful realm on high,
> Where sorrowful moan is all unknown,
> And nothing is born to die?
> The Man in the Moon was tired, it seems,   5
> Of living so long in the land of dreams;
> 'Twas a beautiful sphere, but nevertheless,
> Its lunar life was passionless.
> Unchequer'd by sorrow, undimm'd by crime,
> Untouch'd by the wizard wand of time.   10

---

20 In the first part (published 1839) no mention is made of the Inner Temple.

> 'Twas all too good – there was no scope
> For dread, and of course no room for hope:
> To him the future had no fear,
> To make the present doubly dear;
> The day no cast of coming night,   15
> To make the borrow'd ray more bright;
> And life itself no thought of death,
> To sanctify the boon of breath –
> In short, as we world-people say,
> The Man in the Moon was ennuyé.   20
>
> (anon. 1839. *The Man in the Moon*, p. 3, lines 1-20)

Although Tolkien does not explicitly state that his Man in the Moon[21] is "ennuyé" like the one of the Worcester College Undergraduate (henceforth referred to as 'the anonymous author'), we may infer a similar state of feeling when Tolkien writes that "He [i.e. the Man in the Moon] was tired of his pearls and diamond twirls;" (Tolkien 1983:204-206, l. 13), which actually echoes line 5 above. The Man in the Moon's description of his abode in the anonymous author's poem ("The glad sun lighteth, as of old, / This orbed hall of mine, / With crystal floor, and roof of gold, / And columns argentine;" p. 4, ll. 38-41), too, is strongly reminiscent of Tolkien's poem (Tolkien 1983:204-206, ll. 14-16: "Of his pallid minaret / Dizzy and white at its lunar height / In a world of silver set;"). Yet in spite of all this glory, the anonymous author's Man in the Moon longs for a world of feelings: "To leave awhile this long repose, / And mark, and mingle with the woes / And joys of human life –" (p. 5, ll. 50-52). Tolkien's Man is similarly tired of his lunar world, yet is more discerning in his wishes and longs only for the simple joys of earthly life, such as song and laughter and good food and drink (Tolkien 1983:204-206, ll. 35-38: "How he longed for the mirth of the populous Earth / And the sanguine blood of men; / And coveted song and laughter long / And viands hot and wine"). The descent of the anonymous author's Man in the Moon is worth quoting:

---

21 «Why the Man in the Moon came down too soon»; see Tolkien (1983:204-206). All ensuing references to 'Tolkien's poem' are to this version.

> On such an eve the lunar Sprite
> Toward our planet flew, 70
> And where he went – the firmament
> Seem'd dyed in deeper blue.
> That night full many a mortal eye,
> On heaven's vault did dwell,
> Some mark'd afar a falling star, 75
> But none saw where it fell.
>
> (anon. 1839. *The Man in the Moon*, p. 5, lines 69-75)

Tolkien's Man, too, "fell like meteors do;" (Tolkien 1983:204-206, l. 44). However, the anonymous author's Man in the Moon does not slip and fall tumbling down, as does the one in Tolkien and the nursery rhyme. The anonymous author begins to transform the folk-tradition Man in the Moon into a shining, angel-like, Miltonian 'sprite' with wings. He alights on an island, assumes human form and makes his way into a city where "scarce a thing / Yet told of man's awakening;" (page 7, ll. 103-104; cf. Tolkien's more graphic and down-to-earth description in his poem, Tolkien 1983:204-206, ll. 65-70: "No hearths were laid, not a breakfast made, / And no one would sell him gems; / He found ashes for fire, and his gay desire / For chorus and brave anthems / Met snores instead with all Norfolk abed, / And his round heart nearly broke"). The bells begin to ring at dawn: "From thousand mouths Time's iron tongue / Forth on the startled silence rung, / Telling that truth, too soon forgot, / That while man slumbers – he doth not." (p. 7, ll. 115-117), which parallels Tolkien's less elevated "Though Saint Peter's knell waked many a bell / In the city's ringing towers / To shout the news of his lunatic cruise / In the early morning hours," (Tolkien 1983:204-206, ll. 61-64).

The fact that the anonymous author strives for a 'higher style' becomes obvious from a comparison between these passages and the parallel ones in Tolkien's poem. Furthermore, the poem begins to leave its folk-tale origins behind and the storyline develops into the angel's quest for love in an imperfect, sinful and fallen world. The 'moon-angel' falls for a lady, indeed, and gets to know the sorrows and joys of earthly love. The Angel of Death, then, takes his beloved away and leaves him bereft. No cold plum-porridge there.

The theme of love between immortals and mortals was also of some interest to Tolkien, yet he rather treated it in the framework of the relationship between elves and humans than within the Man-in-the-Moon stories.[22]

Children's books and stories

The figure of the Man in the Moon in the children's books of the late nineteenth and the early twentieth centuries is mostly a harmless and funny figure who 'comes down' from the moon and joins in the adventures of his young companions. This is the case in R's *The Man in the Moon and Other Tales* (1872) and the collection of children's stories entitled *The Man in the Moon or in Days of Old* (1908; The Man-in-the-Moon story is by Nora Pitt-Taylor). It is in the latter collection that the Man in the Moon appears next to but not yet in connection with other popular story-heroes such as Robinson Crusoe, the Sleeping Beauty or the Tin Soldier. The step towards fashioning the Man in the Moon into a character who enters other tale-universes and who interacts with these other protagonists of children's literature is made by Ray Steward in 1905. His book *The Surprising Adventures of the Man in the Moon* presents a rather modern Man in the Moon and his encounters with Santa Claus, Robinson Crusoe, Cinderella and her prince, Jack the Giant Killer, Old Mother Hubbard (all present on the frontispiece, cf. illustration on the opposite page), Little Red Riding Hood, Jack Sprat and others.

---

22 For an additional Man-in-the-Moon poem, see Appendix IV.

Frontispiece, drawn by L.J. Bridgman, for the 1905 edition of Ray M. Stewart's *The Surprising Adventures of the Man in the Moon* (showing the Man in the Moon in company of Santa Claus, Robinson Crusoe, Cinderella and her Prince, Jack the Giant Killer, and Old Mother Hubbard).

The True History of The Man in the Moon and How He Got There (1880) is an exception to the rule. It is a watered down story of Faustus ('Fusticus') who enters a pact with Satan and is banished to the moon when he refuses to hand over his firstborn child to the devil.

6 Some conclusions

Let me try and summarize the main facts and assumptions about the various traditions that are connected with the Man in the Moon. First, the Man in the Moon is someone who has been put onto the moon for punishment. Second, the crime committed is either a theft of some sort or a violation of some religious commandment. Third, the origin of the myth may be traced to the Scandinavian tales about the moon-god Mâni.[23] Fourth, the Man in the Moon developed, from the early seventeenth century onwards, into a proverbial character that occurred more and more often in contexts that no longer had any connection with the original legend(s).

The dominating tradition in England typically present the figure in the moon as a man who carries a thornbush on his back, who is sometimes accompanied by his dog and holds a lantern. The (Italian?) tradition that identifies him with Cain may or may not have been known in England before 1605 and must be considered of minor importance.

Although the evidence looks chaotic and many of the stories and legends cited are either fragmentary or have not been subjected to a critical analysis concerning their possible roots and their relationship with other tales, we can tentatively propose the following theory (cf. Grimm 1883 and Gittée 1901). The Man in the Moon started out as a pagan moon-god, but lost his divine status with his adoption into a Christian context while the central element of 'theft' and the attributes of his 'retinue' (bucket and pole in the account of the *Prose or Younger Edda*, cf. above p. 29) were re-interpreted as fork and bundle (of sticks/thorns). Some tales, then, took these attributes as the starting point to identify him with biblical persons, such as Cain carrying the thorns that he sacrificed instead of the first fruits of his field, the Sabbath-breaker from *Numbers* xv.32-36, Judas Iscariot,[24] or

---

23 Gittée (1901:387) thinks that the popularity of the Man in the Moon legend in England, which has had close links to Scandinavia throughout the Middle Ages, is additional proof for this theory. Also, the classical (mediterranean) tradition has a moon-goddess, and not a male moon-god.

24 Mentioned in Harley (1885:32) as a French superstition. Harley gives no primary source.

with Isaac[25] who carries the bundle of firewood for the sacrifice of himself on Mount Moriah. Other stories provide less 'mythical' explanations for his attributes and the Man in the Moon finds himself as a character of folk-tales that stress either the element of 'theft' or take over the idea of transgression of a divine commandment as the reason for his banishment into the moon. In this context, he may appear as a low life character that is either pitied or laughed at – or both, as in the Middle English poem. After the fifteenth century, he seems to have developed into a clearly identifiable, semi-proverbial character with his traditional attributes of lantern, bundle (of thorns or sticks) on his back, and a dog. Apart from the one appearance in Shakespeare's *A Midsummer Night's Dream*, he is rather the subject of brief references or allusions in plays and songs than a protagonist in his own right. The nonsensical nursery rhymes, then, mark the final phase of his 'descent'.

This rather tumbled ancestry of the nursery rhyme Man in the Moon seems to fall, at least partially, into a pattern. Thus, one could argue that the myth of the children abducted by the moon god Mâni merges into the biblical legends of Cain and the Sabbath-breaker and other non-biblical legends and folk-tales of transgression, or the romance-plot of Basin. These legends, then, merge into the plots of comic folk-poetry and nonsensical nursery rhymes. We may leave it at that for the moment and return to this question once more after an examination of the Man-in-the-Moon motif in Tolkien.

---

25 This interpretation of the Man in the Moon figure is, among others, mentioned by Johannes Praetorius in his *Antropodemvs Plvtonicvs. Das ist / Eine Neue Welt-beschreibung von allerley Wunderbahren Menschen* (1666, chapter XII «Von Mond-Leuten»): "Endlich werden auf solche Art auch Mond-Leute statuiert / wenn nehmlich die albern und abergläubischen Leute vorgeben / dass die schwarze Flecke im Mondlichten / entweder der Mann sey / so am Sabbath-Tage Holtz gelesen / und drüber ist gesteiniget worden: oder dass es Isaac sey / der sein Bündlein Holtz selber auf den Berg Moriam getragen hat zum Menschen-Opffer: Angesehen die Flecke oder Maculae so eine ungefährliche [i.e. approximate] äusserliche Gestalt praesentieren. Oder was sie sich sonsten für eines Menschen Gestalt drinnen einbilden."

7 The Man in the Moon in Tolkien's universe

Preliminary Remark

In order to facilitate the discussion of the occurrence of the Man in the Moon proper in Tolkien's various drafts and versions and to provide a point of reference, I will give first a brief and, as far as possible, chronological list of all the relevant texts. Their relationship is going to be discussed at greater length in the following chapter. For reasons of copyright, I cannot quote the entire poems but have to refer the reader to the (easily) available books by Tolkien.

	title	published	written
1)	«[Why] The Man in the Moon came down too soon»	1923 [1983]	March 1915
2)	«The Man in the Moon came down too soon» (revised and much changed version of number 1)	1962	
3)	«The Cat and the Fiddle: A Nursery Rhyme Undone and its Scandalous Secret Unlocked» (which is an early version of 4)	1923	?
4)	Frodo's Song at the Prancing Pony: «The Man in the Moon Stayed Up Too Late»	1954 & 1962	?
5)	Song by Eriol at Mar Vanwa Tyaliéva (only mentioned in ms, not extant)	———	———
6)	«Uolë and Erinti» (isolated heading without extant story)	———	———
7)	«The Tale of the Sun and Moon» in The Book of Lost Tales	1983	after 1916
8)	Roverandom	1998	1925-1927
9)	«Father Christmas Letter 1927»	1999	1927

A Hobbit Song and a Secret Unlocked

The Man in the Moon is not one of Tolkien's 'high profile' characters. He features neither in *The Silmarillion* nor in *The Hobbit*. Most readers of Tolkien will remember him as one of the characters in Frodo's song[26] at 'The Prancing Pony', which has originally been a poem entitled «The Cat and the Fiddle: A Nursery Rhyme Undone and its Scandalous Secret Unlocked».[27] This poem does not provide much information about the Man in the Moon, except for the fact that he seems to be very fond of good ale. The version discussed is the one found in Book 1, chapter 9 of *The Fellowship of the Ring*, «At the Sign of the Prancing Pony» (*LotR* 174-176; see also *The Adventures of Tom Bombadil*, Poem No. 5 «The Man in the Moon Stayed Up Too Late», pp. 32-35).

Tolkien's introductory remark "only a few words of it are now, as a rule, remembered", is a dig at the nursery rhyme

213

Hey diddle diddle,
The cat and the fiddle
The cow jumped over the moon;[28]
The little dog laughed
To see such sport,
And the dish ran away with the spoon.

(Opie 1997:240, No. 213)

---

26 Christopher Tolkien (in Tolkien 1988:142, fn. 11) writes about the early drafts of the episode containing Frodo's song: "My father first wrote here 'Troll Song', and a rough and unfinished version of it is found in the manuscript at this point. He apparently decided almost at once to substitute 'The Cat and the Fiddle', and there are also two texts of that song included in the manuscript, [...]."
The Hobbitons, a Dutch band, have set the song to music and captured much of its nonsensical exuberance (cf. The Hobbitons. 1996. Song no. 3 on *Songs from Middle-earth*).

27 "'The Cat and the Fiddle', which became Bingo's song at The Prancing Pony, was published in 1923 in Yorkshire Poetry, Vol. II no. 19 (Leeds, the Swan Press)." (Tolkien 1988:145). The text, as found in the original ms, written on Leeds University paper, is reprinted in Tolkien (1988:145-147).

28 For a recent humoristic reference to the cow who jumped over the moon, cf. Appendix V (p. 65).

Illustration to "Hey diddle diddle" by Leslie Brooke (in Lang 1897:193)

Iona and Peter Opie think that this is "[p]robably the best-known nonsense verse in the language" (Opie 1997:240). Tolkien's adaptation and elaboration of this verse provides the 'full story' or, as he announces in the title of his poem, it has "the scandalous secret unlocked". The Man in the Moon's activity is more or less limited to getting drunk and falling under the table and the main focus is, like in the nursery rhyme, on the dancing and playing animals, plates and cutlery. Tolkien's treatment of the Man in the Moon in *The Lord of the Rings* is in many ways comparable to the treatment he received by Shakespeare, Dekker, Jonson or Butler: he is referred to briefly, but no details are given as to his character and background, let alone why he ended up as the Man in the Moon. Shakespeare & Co. could rely on the fact that their audience would make the connection between their allusions and the tradition that goes back at least to the twelfth century. Tolkien's readers, however, have no such tradition to fall back on in the world of Middle-earth – at least initially, that is.

We have to turn to other sources to gain some further information about this lunary character. There exists a rather early poem by Tolkien entitled «The Man in the Moon came down too soon» which he wrote in March 1915 and that was first published in 1923 in *A Northern Venture: Verses by the Members of the Leeds University English School Association*, Leeds: At the Swan Press (Tolkien 1983:202-204 and Hammond 1993:282, B4). It was later collected in a much changed form, together with Frodo's song at 'The Prancing Pony', in *The Adventures of Tom Bombadil* (first published 1962) where it appears as poems No. 6 («The Man in the Moon came down too soon»). This early poem takes the popular nonsensical nursery rhyme about the Man in the Moon as its starting point (cf. p. 12) and, as Shippey (1992:34) writes, it strives to show that the surviving lines are the sorry and garbled survivals of "an ancient story of earthly disillusionment." The text providing the basis for our discussion is the earliest version of the poem as published by Christopher Tolkien in *The Book of Lost Tales: Part I* (Tolkien 1983:204-206).[29]

The poem takes up and answers some of the questions raised by the Middle English «The Man in the Moon» and refers to some of its lines. Thus, we get some information about the Man in the Moon's clothes (l. 5: "Clad in silken robe in his great white globe", cf. ME poem l. 8.), about his longing for fire (l. 25ff.: "And at plenilune in his argent moon / He had wearily longed for Fire – / Not the limpid lights of wan selenites, / But a red terrestrial pyre / With impurpurate glows of crimson and rose / And leaping orange tongue;" cf. ME poem l. 5), and about his dietary habits (l. 39f.: "Eating pearly cakes of light snowflakes / And drinking thin moonshine",

---

29 Christopher Tolkien (Tolkien 1983:204) comments: "The poem about the Man in the Moon exists in many texts, [...]. I give it here in the earlier published form, which was only a little retouched from the earliest workings – where it has the title 'Why the Man in the Moon came down too soon: an East Anglian phantasy'; in the first finished text the title is 'A Faërie: Why the Man in the Moon came down too soon', together with one in Old English: *Se Móncyning*."

cf. ME poem l. 20). The last point, especially in combination with the description of his food cravings (ll. 38-42: "And coveted song and laughter long / And viands hot and wine, / Eating pearly cakes of light snowflakes / And drinking thin moonshine. / He twinkled his feet as he thought of the meat, / Of the punch and the peppery brew"), takes up and parallels the main topic of the ballad-stanzas No. 332a and 332b (cf. pp. 14-15) and Tolkien's "Eating pearly cakes of light snowflakes / And drinking thin moonshine" (ll. 39-40) sounds like a faint echo of Jonson's 'deaw o'th' Moon' (Herford and Simpson 1941, volume 7:519, line 202, cf. Appendix I, p. 60). The parallels to the anonymous poem *The Man in the Moon* (1839 & 1840) have already been pointed out in the discussion of the poem (pp. 35-37).

Neither of the two poems by Tolkien discussed above could be called serious and in this they are true 'spiritual ancestors' of the modern nursery rhymes. They are, however, less nonsensical in so far as they present a series of actions or events, some of which figure as irrational non-sequiturs in nursery rhymes, as part of a (more or less) meaningful narrative. Shippey (1992:35) comments on the relationship between these two poems on the one hand, and the Middle English «The Man in the Moon» and the modern nursery rhymes on the other:

> More significantly, the poem [i.e. the Middle English one] makes one wonder about the unofficial elements of early literary culture. Were there other 'Man in the Moon' poems? Was there a whole genre of sophisticated play on folk-belief? There could have been. Tolkien's 1923 poems attempt to revive it, or invent it, fitting into the gaps between modern doggerel and medieval lyric, creating something that might have existed and would, if it had, account for the jumble and litter of later periods [...].

I think it very likely that Tolkien provides an 'asterisk' reconstruction of a missing linking tradition between medieval and modern Man-in-the-Moon poems. However, his omission of the central 'thornbush' motif raises some questions concerning the exact nature of this link – questions I have no answers for and which may be considered at another time.

The crucial point about Tolkien's Man-in-the-Moon poems is that he uses one of them as Frodo's song. By incorporating «The Cat and the Fiddle» in *The Lord of the Rings*, he makes it a proponent of a Middle-earth Man-in-the-Moon tradition that parallels the one we have encountered in the course of our discussion of the real-world Man-in-the-Moon poems. He thus makes it not merely an 'asterisk' link between the 'real' world nursery rhyme and an allegedly lost late medieval and early modern Man-in-the-Moon folk-poem tradition, but the descendant of an independent Middle-earth tradition.

I am not sure whether Tolkien had been fully aware of all the different versions of the Man-in-the-Moon motif and their possible mutual connections in the 'real' world. He might as well, since the most important articles and books on this topic had been published by the time he had started his academic career. Furthermore, he was familiar with and interested in the theory that postulated a descent or dwindling of myth into legend and then into folk-tale, märchen and nursery tales.[30] Plentiful illustrative examples of such 'dwindling' can be found in every book of nursery rhymes. The following example gives an idea of the kind of far-reaching changes a heroic figure could undergo:

> When good King Arthur ruled this land,
> He was a goodly king;
> He stole three pecks of barley-meal,
> To make a bag-pudding.
>
> A bag-pudding the king did make,
> And stuff'd it well with plums:
> And in it put great lumps of fat,
> As big as my two thumbs.

---

30 Tolkien (1997:123) is skeptical of this pattern if used in order to prove the precedence of nature-myth over all other types of literature.

> The king and queen did eat thereof,
> And noblemen beside;
> And what they could not eat that night,
> The queen next morning fried.
>
> (Lang 1897:32)

The most famous of all British kings is depicted as a meal-thief and hobby-cook, and the first lady of Camelot proves to be a thrifty housewife who does not waste any food but fries the remainder for breakfast. 'Dwindling' indeed.

Yet Tolkien did not follow this lead, and we have been spared any hobbit songs about king Aragorn stealing lembas and lady Arwen frying them for breakfast. What is more likely to have caught Tolkien's eye is the story behind the story of the Man in the Moon as it appears in his two poems. Frodo's song at the 'Prancing Pony' points back to an older mythological tradition on Middle-earth, much in the same way as the nonsensical modern nursery rhymes can be linked to the Old Norse moon god Mâni in our world. In a next chapter, I will therefore try and discuss the various Middle-earth traditions featuring the Man in the Moon and their possible connections.

Sun, Moon and an Elvish Stowaway

The story of the creation of the sun and the moon, as related in the eleventh chapter of *The Silmarillion* («Of the Sun and Moon and the Hiding of Valinor», Tolkien 1994:115-121), gives the following account:

> [The two Trees were poisoned by Ungoliant, and Yavanna tries in vain to heal their mortal wounds.] Yet even as hope failed and her song faltered, Telperion bore at last upon a leafless bough one great flower of silver, and Laurelin a single fruit of gold. [...] But the flower and the fruit Yavanna gave to Aulë, and Manwë hallowed them, and Aulë and his people made vessels to hold them and preserve their radiance [...]. Isil the Sheen the Vanyar of old named the Moon, flower of Telperion in Valinor; [...]. But the Noldor named [it] also Rána, the Wayward, [...]. The maiden whom the Valar chose from among the Maiar to guide the vessel

of the Sun was named Arien, and he that steered the island of the Moon was Tilion. [...] Tilion was a hunter of the company of Oromë, and he had a silver bow. He was a lover of silver, and when he would rest he forsook the woods of Oromë, and going into Lórien he lay in dream by the pools of Estë, in Telperion's flickering beams; and he begged to be given the task of tending for ever the last Flower of Silver. [...] Isil was first wrought and made ready, and first rose into the realm of the stars, and was the elder of the new lights, as was Telperion of the Trees. [Next the vessel of Arien is launched.] Now Varda purposed that the two vessels should journey in Ilmen and ever be aloft, but not together; each should pass from Valinor into the east and return, the one issuing from the west as the other turned from the east. [...] But Tilion was wayward and uncertain in speed, and held not to his appointed path; and he sought to come near to Arien, being drawn by her splendour, though the flame of Anar scorched him, and the island of the Moon was darkened. [Because of this, among other reasons, Varda changed the course of the Sun and the Moon, so that the Sun would now be drawn into the waters of the Outer Sea in the evening and transported east underneath the Earth, so as to rise from there in the morning.] Varda commanded the Moon to journey in like manner, and passing under Earth to arise in the east, but only after the Sun had descended from heaven. But Tilion went with uncertain pace, as yet he goes, and was still drawn towards Arien, as he shall ever be; so that often both may be seen above the Earth together, or at times it will chance that he comes so nigh that his shadow cuts off her brightness and there is darkness amid the day.
(Tolkien 1994:116-119)

This tale of the creation of the moon and the sun is primarily an aetiological account[31] that provides answers to such (implicit) questions as 'How were they created?', 'Which of the two is the older?', 'Why do they disappear in the west and rise in the east?', 'Why are there 'shadows' or 'spots' on the

---

31 The earliest version of this creation myth, «The Tale of the Sun and Moon» in *The Book of Lost Tales: Part I*, is introduced by a frame story in which Eriol asks his host: "'Whence be the Sun and Moon, O Lindo? [...].'" (Tolkien 1983:174) and thus triggers the tale.

moon?', 'Why is the course of the moon not as regular as that of the sun?', and 'How does an eclipse of the sun come about?'. The moon, once called 'the island of the moon', is depicted as a 'vessel' that is 'steered' by Tilion, a Maia (i.e. one of the spirits that serve the Valar).[32] Thus, the general idea we get is that of the moon as a kind of vessel or floating island[33] that contains the Flower of Telperion which gives forth the silver light, and is steered by Tilion on its way across the heavens. The marks on the moon are the result of a 'close encounter' with the sun during which it got scorched.

The possible connections to Tolkien's two Man-in-the-Moon poems are tenuous. The concept of the moon as a kind of vessel with a steersman or driver occurs in Frodo's song, though there the 'ship-vessel' has become a horse-drawn cart which might be more easily linked to the Old Norse moon chariot as it appears in Snorri Sturluson's *Edda* (cf. p. 29). Also, allusion is made to the waywardness of the moon, no longer caused by a yearning for the splendour of the sun, but rather by an overfondness of ale. Yet the story, as it appears in the posthumously published *The Silmarillion*, is an edited version "constituted from two later versions not greatly dissimilar the one from the other" (Tolkien 1983:200), as Christopher Tolkien comments. In his «Foreword» to *The Silmarillion* (Tolkien 1994:8), he mentions that he had chosen to work out a single text by means of selecting and arranging the available material into, as far as possible, a coherent and internally self-consistent narrative. Thus, the only text available in printed form until the publication of *The Book of Lost Tales: Part I* in 1983, was based on two "later versions [that] read in places almost as summaries of the early story" (Tolkien 1983:200). It is this longer and more elaborate 'early story', published as «The Tale of the Sun and Moon»

---

32 If we take the Valar as corresponding to one class of the Epiphania which comprises the three highest orders of angels (Thrones, Cherubim, Seraphim) in the ninefold division of the heavenly hosts, then the Maiar can be compared to one of the lesser ranks of angels.

33 The moon appears as a floating 'island' in a picture from Tolkien's *The Book of Ishness* (No. 45 in Hammond and Scull 1995:49). Hammond and Scull comment: "[The picture] shows the Man in the Moon, with a long beard and tall hat, sliding earthwards on a thread. In the poem he falls 'like meteors do' into the ocean and is taken by boat to Norwich, so the 'spidery hair' points towards East Anglia. One can identify the British Isles, Europe, India, Africa, and North America on the Earth; but there are unfamiliar continents in the Atlantic and Pacific Oceans, presumably Atlantis and Lemuria."

in *The Book of Lost Tales* (Tolkien 1983:174-206), that sheds additional light on the relationship between the two Man-in-the-Moon poems and the account of the creation of the sun and the moon. Tolkien started writing *The Book of Lost Tales* in 1916-17 (Tolkien 1983:8) and left it, incomplete, several years later. We can therefore assume that the tales and poems collected in this book originated in close temporal vicinity of the two Man-in-the-Moon poems. Indeed, the account of the shaping of the vessel of the sun and the vessel of the moon contains some details as well as some general characteristics that suggest that this version is closer to the two poems than the later account in *The Silmarillion*. Thus, "The white horses of the Moon" («The Man in the Moon Stayed Up Too Late.», l. 37) are obviously an echo of the "wild white horses" that launched the Ship of the Moon in «The Tale of the Sun and Moon»: "Slower was the wayfaring [of the Ship of the Moon] than the lifting of the Ship of Morn, and all the folk strain lustily at the ropes, until Oromë coming harnesses thereto a herd of wild white horses, and thus comes the vessel to the topmost place" (Tolkien 1983:194). The main points of this early story can be summarized as follows: After Ungoliant's poisoning of the Trees, Yavanna tries to heal them in vain. Yet Vána's tears prompt Laurelin to bring forth golden blossoms and one huge golden fruit. Aulë fashions the Ship of the Sun out of this fruit. Some days later, Silpion (~Telperion in the later accounts) produces a huge flower, 'The Rose of Silpion'. It grows so heavy that the bough snaps and it falls to the ground, so that some of its petals are crushed and tarnished. This incident accounts for the markings on the face of the moon and is at variance with the explanation given in *The Silmarillion* (cf. above). Aulë, then, builds the Ship of the Moon:

> Of *vírin* now he built a marvellous vessel, and often have men spoken of the Ship of the Moon, yet is it scarce like to any bark that sailed or sea or air. Rather was it like an island of pure glass, albeit not very great, and tiny lakes there were bordered with snowy flowers that shone, for the water of those pools that gave them sap was the radiance of Telimpë. Midmost of that shimmering isle was wrought a cup of that crystalline stuff that Aulë made and therein the magic Rose was set, and the glassy body of the vessel sparkled wonderfully as it gleamed therein.

> Rods there were and perchance they were of ice, and they rose upon it like aëry masts, and sails were caught to them by slender threads, and Uinen wove them of white mists and foam, and some were sprent with glinting scales of silver fish, some threaded with tiniest stars like points of light – sparks caught in snow when Nielluin was shining.
> (Tolkien 1983:192)

The splendour of this 'crystal island' is reminiscent of the description of the Man in the Moon's abode in the poem «The Man in the Moon Came Down Too Soon». And indeed, he makes his appearance about a dozen lines further down in the text:

> Manwë bade therefore Ilinsor, a spirit of the Súruli who loved the snows and the starlight and aided Varda in many of her works, to pilot this strange-gleaming boat, and with him went many another spirit of the air arrayed in robes of silver and white, or else of palest gold; but an aged Elf with hoary locks stepped upon the Moon unseen and hid him in the Rose, and there dwells he ever since and tends that flower, and a little white turret has he builded on the Moon where often he climbs and watches the heavens, or the world beneath, and that is Uolë Kúvion who sleepeth never. Some indeed have named him the Man in the Moon, but Ilinsor is it rather who hunts the stars. [...] and whiles again he [the Moon] sails serenely to the West, and up through the pure lucency of his frame the wide Rose of Silpion is seen, and some say the aged form of Uolë Kúvion beside.
> (Tolkien 1983:192-92)

Thus, we find the Man in the Moon, complete with his "palid minaret" or "little white turret", at the very inception of Tolkien's universe: a stowaway on the heavenly Ship of the Moon.

It seems that Tolkien was quite clear about the distinction between Tilion/Ilinsor, the steersman of the moonship, and the Man in the Moon. In this he is close to the medieval and later tradition which likewise distinguishes between the moon god(dess) and the Man in the Moon who is not so much a descendant of a divine figure, but rather a figure that exists next to and independent of a moon god(dess).

Yet the presence of such a figure as the Man in the Moon in Tolkien's work has been felt as something of a problem, or at least an irritation. Christopher Tolkien comments: "The aged Elf Uolë Kúvion [...] seems almost to have strayed in from another conception; his presence gives difficulty in any case, since we have just been told [...] that Silmo could not sail in the Moonship because he was not of the children of the air and could not 'cleanse his being of its earthwardness'." (Tolkien 1983:202). Admittedly, there is a logical incoherence in this passage, but I do not think that it is that which makes him so ill at ease with the figure of Uolë Kúvion. A truer reason for Christopher Tolkien's (covert) objection against the inclusion of such a character can be inferred from his commentary on a note in one of Tolkien's pocket-books which

> refers to a poem 'The Man in the Moon' which is to be sung by Eriol, 'who says he will sing them a song of a legend touching Uolë Mikúmi [the earlier name of Uolë Kúvion] as Men have it'. My father wrote a poem about the Man in the Moon in March 1915 [i.e. «The Man in the Moon Came Down Too Soon.»], but if it was this that he was thinking of including it would have startled the company of Mar Vanwa Tyaliéva – and he would have had to change its references to places in England which were not yet in existence. Although it is very probable that he had something quite different in mind, I think it may be of interest to give this poem in an early form.
> (Tolkien 1983:202)

It becomes clear from this comment that the Man in the Moon is thought of as a rather embarassing 'low folk element' that jars with the general elevated 'mythic' tone of the august assembly at Mar Vanwa Tyaliéva. He simply does not fit in, at least from Christopher Tolkien's point of view. The true reason for his reserve shown towards the Man in the Moon is thus not to be sought in the minor problems of place-names, that would have to be adjusted, or other logical inconsistencies that the presence of such a character creates in a mythic story. Of course, it is tempting to see the Man in the Moon as an intruder, a stray element that will be omitted from the mythic account of the creation of the sun and the moon in the later stages and given its appropriate place in a children's story such as *Roverandom*, where he appears as an old, bearded wizard who dwells in a white tower and is accompanied by a moon-dog.[34] In the «Letter from Father Christmas» for 1927 (Tolkien 1999:32-35), Father Christmas tells about the Man in the Moon's visit to the North Pole. He is entertained with plum pudding and brandy and in order to warm the guest's cold fingers, the North Polar Bear plays 'snapdragon' with the Man in the Moon – who promptly burns his fingers.

It is understandable that Christopher Tolkien felt rather ill at ease with the prospect of a possible incorporation of an entire poem like «The Man in the Moon Came Down Too Soon» into the narrative frame of the mythic tale-collection. Yet Tolkien may not have shared his scruples and might not have hesitated to combine 'high mythic' characters, such as the Maiar, with 'low mythic' ones, such as the aged Elf who is explicitly mentioned to be thought of by some to be the Man in the Moon. Yet Tolkien was careful not to create too much of a dissonance and allowed Uolë Kúvion no more than a few lines. He merely introduced the figure of the Man in the Moon without developing his comic potential within the mythic tale. Also, an "isolated heading 'Uolë and Erinti' in the little pocket-book used among things for suggestions of stories to be told [...] no doubt implies that a tale was preparing on the subject of Uolë;" (Tolkien 1983:202). This points towards an intended mythical 'upgrading' of Uolë Kúvion, and had this tale ever been written, it would probably have provided us with a deeper understanding of the character of the Man in the Moon. Such as things are, it has become yet another tantalising hint of 'depth' of tales lost or untold.

The later texts that deal with the creation of the sun and moon no longer mention Uolë Kúvion. He 'strays out' of the account of the creation of the sun and moon proper and resurges only sporadically in a Middle-earth context, such as in the planned but not extant song by Eriol and the one by Frodo at 'The Prancing Pony', but he figures more prominently in other works such as *Roverandom* and *The Father Christmas Letters*.

---

34 This story was written largely between 1925 and 1927. It also provides accounts for the lunar eclipses and other phenomena connected with the moon. Scull and Hammond give a competent discussion of the story's development in the introduction to their 1998 edition of *Roverandom*.

Did the Man in the Moon Really Come Down?

I have mentioned before, in the context of our discussion of the medieval and subsequent Man-in-the-Moon tradition(s), that the surviving evidence may be interpreted as a 'descent' from myth to folk-tale and nursery rhyme. The question arises as to whether it would be possible to see a similar development in the Man-in-the-Moon motif in Tolkien.

The evidence available does not favour such a theory of descent, but rather the contrary. The 'low mythic' elements are present right from the beginning. The Man in the Moon is not a dwindled down version of Tilion/Ilinsor, but he is extant in the form of Uolë Kúvion at the very inception of Tolkien's mythic universe. And I think that neither this 'inclusion' of a low mythic element nor Tolkien's idea to have Eriol recite «The Man in the Moon Came Down Too Soon» were merely passing fads. Tolkien himself, about a quarter of a century after the composition of the first Man-in-the-Moon poem, rendered explicit some of his beliefs about and attitudes on the question of 'high and low mythologies' in his Andrew Lang lecture of 1939, which was later published as «On Fairy-Stories». He argues against the theory of a gradual descent from (nature-)myth to epic and heroic legend, and from those to folk-tales, märchen, fairy-stories and nursery-tales (Tolkien 1997:123). Tolkien points out that there "is no fundamental distinction between the higher and lower mythologies. Their people live, if they live at all, by the same life, just as in the mortal world do kings and peasants." (Tolkien 1997:123). If it were not so, we ought to feel very ill at ease with such an account as the *Thrymskvitha* (to be found in the *Elder Edda*, cf. also Gordon 1927:118-123) where Thórr, one of the rulers of the Norse world, is shown in a not very dignified light.[35] Tolkien was aware of this and, as his discussion of the *Thrymskvitha* shows (Tolkien

---

35 The plot is simple: Thórr's hammer has been stolen by the giant Thrymr who asks to be given Freya in exchange for the hammer. Thórr dresses up as a woman and, accompanied by Loki, pretends to be Freya. He draws the attention and suspicion of the husband-in-spe at the wedding-banquet since he devours an enormous amount of food. Loki always saves the situation by providing answers for the 'bride's' enormous appetite. After the feast, Thórr's hammer is given to the 'bride' as the bridal gift and Thórr kills all the giants present with his hammer.

1997:124), he did not deem it incompatible with the more 'elevated' narratives in the same collection. Problems arise only "if you insist that one of these things must precede the other" (Tolkien 1997:124), i.e. if you cannot allow for peaceful cohabitation of 'high' and 'low' mythologies. Applied to our case, one could say that there is no fundamental distinction between the rather dignified mythology of the gods of Middle-earth and the more 'folksy' one of the Man in the Moon.

Let us return for a moment to our discussion of the references to the Man in the Moon from Neckam to Shakespeare and to the nursery rhymes, and let us reconsider the evidence in the light of our findings in Tolkien. Does not the first explicit reference to the Man in the Moon, that of Alexander Neckam, exhibit a similar structure to Tolkien's earliest tale of the sun and the moon in presenting 'high mythology' (in Neckam's case: pseudo-biblical mythology) next to 'low mythology'? And is not Henryson's depiction of Lady Cynthia with the Man in the Moon painted on her dress a most striking example of such co-habitation? The postulated 'descent' must therefore have taken place, if ever, some time before the first explicit mentioning of the Man in the Moon and cannot be backed by any written evidence. Yet if we take Tolkien's model of "the Cauldron of Story, [that] has always been boiling, and to it have continually been added new bits" (Tolkien 1997:125) then we need no longer worry about (minor) inconsistencies and new and unexplicable combinations of motifs and narrative elements both in Tolkien's work and the real world. We have, instead of a linear descent or ascent, a randomised pattern of mixed combinations that does at the same time allow limited regular development. Such a 'model' is much more suitable to accomodate a host of sometimes contradictory characters, such as we have encountered on our exploration of the Man of the Moon tradition. Mâni, Bil and Hiuki, Cain, Isaac, Lady Cynthia, Basin of the Charlemagne chansons de geste, the Sabbath-breaker, the thorn-thief, the enigmatic hosed magpie Hubert, the various transgressors against a divine commandment, and the lover of (cold) plumpudding in the ballads and nursery rhymes – they all have found themselves attached for a longer or shorter period to the motif of the Man in the Moon while floating in the Cauldron of Story. The modern example par excellence of such an amalgamation of characters and stories is Steward's *The Surprising Adventures of the Man in the Moon* (1905; cf. pp. 38-39), though he overdoes things a bit. Tolkien's treatment of the Man-in-the-Moon motif in his works may be seen in the light of his concept of the Cauldron of Story. His multiple versions and variations of the same story, often related from different points of views (Elf or Man), his reworkings and revisions may not be seen as aiming at a final unified version, but rather at creating an impression of depth and richness that rivals its parallel tradition in our world.

III Conclusion

My study has been concerned with a moteley collection of songs, poems, tales, sketches, notes and references that cluster around the figure of the Man in the Moon. The nonsensical nursery rhymes which provided the inspiration for Tolkien's poems «The Cat and the Fiddle» (better known under the title «The Man in the Moon Stayed Up Too Late») and «The Man in the Moon came down too soon» have become the starting points for an exploratory journey into the (not always logical and coherent) development of high and low mythologies that have grown around this character in both the real world and Middle-earth. On the level of 'high mythology', the Man in the Moon as a figure from the myths of the Germanic tradition (Mâni) finds his counterpart in Tolkien's mythological accounts of the creation of the ships of the Sun and the Moon (Tilion). One step further down, we find real-world tales about the Man in the Moon that present him as an unlucky mortal who was banished onto the moon as punishment for some transgression. This corresponds, more or less, to Tolkien's figure of Uolë Kúvion, the aged Elf, who hid himself on the Ship of the Moon and who has been living there ever since. Finally, the numerous real-world ballads and nursery rhymes that feature the Man in the Moon and that inspired the later developments in poetry and children's literature, find an equivalent in Tolkien's Man-in-the-Moon poems and his children's story *Roverandom*. Thus, the complex and often contradictory depiction of the Man in the Moon in the real world is matched by a likewise intricately woven (and often contradictory) tradition of the Man-in-the-Moon figure in Tolkien's universe. Tolkien's multi-layered treatment of the motif imbues it with a complexity and depth that needs not shun any comparison with the real-world tradition that looks back over eight centuries.

The 'gleaning' is done, and the reader may turn to the bibliography to see in whose fields I have been busy gleaning. I hope that the close examination of a hitherto neglected instance of 'structural depth' has provided some deeper insights into this aspect of Tolkien's work. I also hope that we have caught a glimpse of what lies beyond and that we may see a bit farther than our predecessors on whose shoulders we stand.

Appendix I

Additional examples of the medieval tradition transformed

Additional Shakespearean references to the Man in the Moon may be found in *The Tempest* (2.2.129-133; Greenblatt 1997:3081),[36] and *Love's Labour's Lost* (5.2.211-214; Greenblatt 1997:784).[37]

Thomas Dekker (c.1570 - c.1641), a contemporary of Shakespeare's, dedicates the eighth chapter of his *Lanthorne and Candle-light* (1609), an account of the metropolitan demi-monde, to 'Moone men' and writes the following:

> A *Moone-man* signifies in English, a mad-man, because the Moone hath greatest domination (aboue any other Planet) ouer the bodies of Frantick persons. [...] And as in the Moone there is a man, that neuer stirres without a bush of thornes at his

---

36 *Caliban*: Hast thou not dropped from heaven? / *Stefano*: Out o'th'moon, I do assure thee. I was the man i'th' / moon when time was. / *Caliban*: I have seen thee in her, and I do adore thee. / My mistress showed me thee, and thy dog and thy bush. (*The Tempest* 2.2.129-133; Greenblatt 1997:3081).

37 *Rosaline*: [...] Not yet? – no dance! Thus change I like the moon. / *King*: Will you not dance? How come you thus estranged? / *Rosaline*: You took the moon at full, but now she's changed. / *King*: Yet still she is the moon, and I the man. (*Love's Labour's Lost* 5.2.211-214; Greenblatt 1997:784).

backe, so these *Moone-men* lie vnder bushes, & are indeed no better then Hedge creepers.[38] [...] By a by-name they are called Gipsies,[39] they call themselues Egiptians, others in mockery call them *Moone-men*

(Grosart 1885, volume 3:258-259)

Some eleven years later, the Man in the Moon and his attributes are the subject of a conversation in Ben Jonson's (1573-1637) masque *News from the New World discovered in the Moon* (performed 1620, printed 1640):

1 Herald:	Who [i.e. Poetry] after a world of these curious uncertainties, hath employed thither a servant of hers in search of truth: who has been there –
2 Herald:	In the Moone.
1 Herald:	In person.
Factor:	Where? which is he? I must see his Dog at his girdle, and the bush of thornes at his backe, ere I beleeve it.
1 Herald:	Do not trouble your faith then, for if that bush of thornes should prove a goodly Grove of Okes; in what case were you, and your expectation?
2 Herald:	Those are stale Ensignes o'the Stages man i'th' Moone, deliverd downe to you by musty Antiquitie, and are as doubtfull credit as the makers.

(Herford and Simpson 1941, volume 7:516-517, lines 105-118)

In this example, the traditional folk belief in the Man in the Moon is juxtaposed with and then corrected by the more scientific idea that the marks on the moon are landscape features and that the real 'men in the

---

38 'Hedge creepers' are rogues.
39 Some traditions believe the Gypsies to be the descendants of Cain who has been condemned to wander the world without finding a permanent abode (*Genesis* 4:14).This would seem to be yet another indirect and circumstantial point of evidence for Emerson's (1906b) argument that the 'English' Man in the Moon has to be identified with Cain. Yet the fact that Dekker does not refer to Cain at all must be seen as an even stronger argument against Emerson's theory. For a discussion of the Cain – Man in the Moon problem see pp. 23-26 of this paper.

moon' are rational beings. However, their dietary habits are about as strange, or even stranger, than the ones of the traditional Man in the Moon:

> *Factor*:   How doe they live then?
> *1 Herald*:   O'th' deaw o'th' Moone like Grasshoppers [...]
> (Herford and Simpson 1941, volume 7:519, lines 201-202)

Jonson may echo Lucian of Samosata's *Icaromenippus* (2 cent. A.D.; cf. Harmon 1915), which had been translated by Thomas Morus (1478-1535). Lucian's narrator Menippus travels to the moon, and subsequently to the halls of the gods, with the help of the wing of a vulture on his left, and that of an eagle on his right arm. On the moon, he meets Empedocles who had thrown himself into the crater of Aetna but was carried up to the moon where he "walk[s] the air a great deal, and [...] live[s] on dew." (Harmon 1915:291).

The next example comes from Samuel Butler's (1612-1680) *Hudibras* (1663). Hudibras, in the second part, canto III, lines 733-790, philosophises about the nature of heaven, the sun and, especially, the moon and its alleged inhabitants and provocatively asks his readers:

> But what, alas, is it to us,
> Whether in the *Moon*, men thus, or thus,
> Do eat their *Porredg*,[40] cut their Corns,
> Or whether they have Tayls or Horns?
> [...]
> Or does the *Man* i'th' *Moon* look big,
> And wear a huger *Perewig*,
> Shew in his gate, or face, more tricks
> Then our own *Native Lunaticks*?
> (Wilders 1967:173-174, lines 745-748 & 767-770)

---

40 This may be a conscious allusion to tradition that depicts the Man in the Moon eating either 'cold plum porridge' or 'hot pease-porridge'; this tradition has survived in the nursery rhymes.

Appendix II

Social and political satirical works

Godwin's *The Man in the Moone* provided the model for Cyrano de Bergerac's (1619-1655) *Les Estats et Empires de la Lune* (manuscript c. 1648, publication 1657; cf. Lachèvre 1968, volume 1:5-99), which can be seen as uniting Godwinian travelogue and the more pronounced political and social satires which used 'The Man in the Moon' in the title or as a pseudonym, but which had often only a very tenuous – or even non-existent – connection to the traditional Man-in-the-Moon figure. Thus, in 1609, an anonymous work with the title *The Man in the Moone telling strange Fortunes; or, The English Fortune Teller* (republished in Halliwell 1849) was published in London. It is an early example of the numerous social satirical tracts that will follow and it deals not with the Man in the Moon at all, but with various set characters (the drunkard, the tobacconist, the virgin, the wanton wife, etc.) who appear before the 'fortune teller' with the rather unlikely name Fido (who may be, as the title implies, the Man in the Moon) and his retinue. Fido, then, 'analyses' each of his customers in turn and predicts for them their respective fortunes. Several decades later (in 1657) an author, hiding himself behind the initials (?) S.S., published a poem entitled *The Man in the Moone Discovering a World of Knavery under the Sunne* in which he then relates the 'knaveries' of various professions and classes. A poem with a very similar title was anonymously published three years later: *The Man in the Moone Discovering a World of Knavery under the Sun. With sundry memorable Accidents, and strange proceedings both in City, Town, Court and Country; and many delightful passages touching divers upstart and Tyrannical TRAYTORS*. The narrator introduces the Man in the Moon as his informer in the opening lines of the poem: "As I was walking up and down / the Man in the Moon did call, / And told me what in ev'ry Town / and City did befall," thus presenting a political satire. Satirical, social and political tracts had obviously taken a predilection to the Man in the Moon and we find quite a number that feature the Man in the Moon in the title, be it as informer, or as author. I list only a selection of these works: Philagatus' *The Informer's Doom: Or, an amazing and seasonable letter from Utopia, directed to the Man in the Moon* (1683), the anonymously published *The Regular Physician: Or, Make Hay while the Sun shines. A poem by the Man in the Moon* (1715), Thomson's *The Man in the Moon; Or, Travels into the Lunar Regions by the Man of the People* (1783), the anonymous *London unmask'd: Or The New Town Spy. By the Man in the Moon* (1784), and William Hone's pamphlets with the titles *The Man in the Moon* and *The Loyal Man in the Moon* (1820; cf. Rickword 1971:83-134).

Scientific works

Thus, while the traditional figure of the Man in the Moon was still present in works of political satire, although he had lost his attributes and become a mere cipher,[41] he had disappeared more or less completely from works dealing with the scientific exploration of the moon. If he is mentioned at all, then it is in an aside about popular superstitions – as was already the case in Alexander Neckam in the twelfth century. John Wilkins (1638:103) refers to him 'en passant' in his discussion of the spots of the moon and also mentions the three most prominent traditions of the Man in the Moon:[42]

> As for the forme of those spots, some of the vulgar thinke thay represent a man, and the Poets guesse 'tis the boy Endimion, whose company shee loves so well, that shee carries him with her, others will have it onely to be the face of a man as the Moone is usually pictured[.]

---

41 The use of 'The Man in the Moon' for naming pubs and his appearance on pub-signs and shop bills (cf. illustration from Harley 1885:12 on p. 14) may be seen as further examples of this development. Maclaren's play *The Man in the Moon* (1815), then, takes his title from the taproom 'at the sign of the Moon' where a major part of the action takes place. The patrons, in one scene (Maclaren 1815:12), make fun of a drunken baloon traveller and pretend that he has actually arrived on the moon.

42 Wilkins also mentions the moon-calf, which reappears in Tolkien as the cow that jumped over the moon (Wilkins 1638:113): "And if a whirle-winde did chance to snatch any thing up, and afterwards raine it downe againe, the ignorant multitude are apt to believe that it dropt from Heaven. Thus Avicenna related the story of a Calfe which fell downe in a storme, the beholders thinking it a Moon-calfe, and that it fell thence."

Appendix III

The Man in the Moon in idiomatic and proverbial expressions

According to the *Oxford English Dictionary* (vol. 9, p. 318, 'man in the moon'), the man in the moon occurs since the middle of the sixteenth century in the proverbial phrase 'no more than the man in the moon', meaning 'not at all'. And since the end of the sixteenth century, the expression 'the man in the moon' is used to refer to an imaginary person. "In recent use, [it has become] a jocular name for a pretendedly unknown person who supplies money for illicit expenditure at elections." (*OED* vol. 9:318). This side-development, however, has remained without influence on the imaginative perception of the person of the Man in the Moon.

Appendix IV

A more recent example of a Man-in-the-Moon poem is by Reverend Thomas Pittaway and was published in a small volume of poems in 1934.

The Man in the Moon

I look on the earth
With languid eye,
Bewailing my birth,
Wishing to die;
For I am alone,   5
An elderly man,
My joy overthrown,
My cheek so wan:
O come to me soon,
Some one from earth: 10
The man in the moon
Bewails his birth.

I live in the cold,
I feed on frost,
My soul I have sold,   15
And I am lost;
I wander about,
Where no one goes,
I am always out,
With freezing toes: 20
O come to me soon,
Some one from earth:
The man in the moon
Bewails his birth.

Does no one befriend   25
A soul out cast?
And will no one end
My lenten fast?
Will you mock my smile,
So hard and grim?   30
I have looked long while,
Till sight is dim:
O come to me soon,
Some one from earth:
The man in the moon   35
Bewails his birth.

(Pittaway 1934:1)

This poem steers clear of the 'undergraduate of Worcester College's' Miltonian pathos and may be seen as harking back to the tradition that sees the Man in the Moon as a sinner who has been banished into the moon for his crime.

Appendix V

Cow by Bestie (Paperlink 1994; reproduced by permission)

THOMAS HONEGGER holds a Ph.D. from the University of Zurich. He is the author of *From Phoenix to Chauntecleer: Medieval English Animal Poetry* (1996) and has edited several volumes with essays on medieval literature and numerous books on Tolkien. Apart from his publications on animals and Tolkien, he has written about Chaucer, Shakespeare, and mediaeval romance. He is Professor for English Mediaeval Studies at the Friedrich-Schiller-University (Jena, Germany). Homepage: http://www2.uni-jena.de/fsu/anglistik/homepage/Honegger3.htm

References

ANDERSON, Douglas A. (ed.). 2002. *The Annotated Hobbit*. Revised and expanded edition. Boston: Houghton Mifflin.

ANON. 1609. *The Man in the Moone telling strange Fortunes; or, The English Fortune Teller*. London: Printed by I.W. for Nathaniel Butter. Reprinted in Halliwell 1849.

ANON. 1660. *The Man in the Moone Discovering a World of Knavery under the Sun. With sundry memorable Accidents, and strange proceedings both in City, Town, Court and Country; and many delightful passages touching divers upstart and Tyrannical TRAYTORS*. London: Printed for John Johnson.

ANON. 1715. *The Regular Physician: Or, Make Hay while the Sun shines. A poem by the Man in the Moon*. London: Printed and sold by EDM. Powell.

ANON. 1784. *London unmask'd: Or The New Town Spy. By the Man in the Moon*. London: Printed for William Adlard.

ANON. 1839/1840. *The Man in the Moon. A Poem*. Part the First 1839. By an Undergraduate of Worcester College, London. Part the Second 1840. By an Undergraduate of Worcester College, London, and the Inner Temple, London. Oxford: Printed for the author by D. A. Talboys.

ANON. 1880. *The True History of The Man in the Moon and How He Got There*. London: W. Swan Sonnenschein & Allen.

ANON. 1908. *The Man in the Moon or in Days of Old*. London: Dean & Son.

ANON. 1913. *The Man in the Moon: A Nursery Rhyme Picture Book*. With drawings by Leslie Brooke. London and New York: Frederick Warne & Co.

BABINGTON, Churchill (ed.). 1860. *Reginald Pecock: The Repressor of Over Much Blaming of the Clergy*. Two volumes. Rolls Series. London: Longman, Green, Longman, and Roberts.

BARING-GOULD, S. 1906. *Curious Myths of the Middle Ages*. New (2nd?) edition. 1st edition 1866. London, New York and Bombay: Longmans, Green and Co.

BENNET, J.A.W. and G.V. SMITHERS (eds.). 1974. *Early Middle English Verse and Prose*. 2nd edition 1968, reprinted with corrections 1974. 1st edition 1966. Oxford: At the Clarendon Press.

BENSON, Larry D. (ed.). 1987. *The Riverside Chaucer*. 3rd edition, based on *The Works of Geoffrey Chaucer* edited by F.N. Robinson. Oxford: Oxford University Press.

BEVINGTON, David (ed.). 1996. *Endymion: John Lyly*. (1588) The Revels Plays. Manchester and New York: Manchester University Press.

BUTLER, John Antony (ed.). 1995. *Bishop Francis Godwin: The Man in the Moon*. Publications of the Barnabe Riche Society No. 3. Ottawa: Dovehouse Editions.

CARPENTER, Humphrey. 1977. *J.R.R. Tolkien – A Biography*. London: George Allen & Unwin.

CAWLEY, A.C. (ed.). 1958. *The Wakefield Pageants in the Towneley Cycle*. Old and Middle English Texts. Manchester: Manchester University Press.

DAVIES, R.T. (ed.). 1963. *Medieval English Lyrics*. London: Faber and Faber.

EMERSON, Oliver F. 1906a. «'Cain' and the Moon.» *The Athenæum* No. 4112 (August 18, 1906):186-87.

- - -. 1906b. «Legends of Cain, Especially in Old and Middle English.» *Publications of the Modern Language Association (PMLA)* 21:831-929.

FAULKES, Antony (ed. and trans.). 1987. *Snorri Sturluson: Edda*. Everyman's Library. London and Melbourne: Dent.

FOX, Denton (ed.). 1968. *Robert Henryson: Testament of Cresseid*. London and Edinburgh: Nelson.

FRYE, Northrop. 1957. *Anatomy of Criticism: Four Essays*. Princeton, N.J.: Princeton University Press.

FURNIVALL, Frederick J. (ed.). 1868. *Caxton's Book of Curtesye*. Early English Text Society Original Series No. 32. London: Trübner.

GITTEE, A. 1901. «De Legende van het Mannetje uit de Maan.» *Taal en Letteren* 11:386-406.

GORDON, E.V. 1927. *An Introduction to Old Norse*. Oxford: At the Clarendon Press.

GREENBLATT, Stephen, Walter COHEN, Jean E. HOWARD and Katharine EISAMAN MAUS (eds.). 1997. *The Norton Shakespeare*. Based on the Oxford Edition. New York and London: W.W. Norton & Co.

GRIMM, Jacob. 1883. *Teutonic Mythology*. Three volumes. Volume 2. Translated from the 4th edition (1875-78, edited by Elard Hugo Meyer) by James Steven Stallybrass. First German edition Göttingen 1835. London: George Bell & Sons.

GROSART, Alexander B. (ed.). 1885. *Thomas Dekker: Lanthorne and Candle-Light*. Originally published 1609. Republished in: *The Non-Dramatic Works of Thomas Dekker*. Four volumes. Volume 3, pp. 171-304. London: Hazell, Watson, and Viney.

HALL, James. 1974. *Dictionary of Subjects and Symbols in Art*. London: John Murray.

HALLIWELL, James Orchard (ed.). 1849. *Notices of Fugitive Tracts, and Chap-Books*. London: Printed for the Percy Society by Richards.

- - - (ed.). 1970. *Popular Rhymes & Nursery Tales of England*. 1st edition ?. London, Sydney and Toronto: The Bodley Head.

HAMMOND, Wayne G., with the assistance of Douglas A. ANDERSON. 1993. *J.R.R. Tolkien: A Descriptive Bibliography*. Winchester: St Paul's Bibliographies / New Castle, Delaware: Oak Knoll Books.

- - - and Christina SCULL. 1995. *J.R.R. Tolkien: Artist and Illustrator*. London: HarperCollins.

HARLEY, Timothy. 1885. *Moon Lore*. London: Swan Sonnenschein, Le Bas & Lowrey.

HARMON, A.H. (ed. and trans.). 1915. *Lucian*. Seven volumes. The Loeb Classical Library. London: William Heinemann.

HEBEL, William J. (ed.). 1931. *The Works of Michael Drayton*. Five volumes. Oxford: At the Shakespeare Head Press.

HERFORD, C.H. and Percy and Evelyn SIMPSON. 1941. *Ben Jonson: The Sad Shepherd, The Fall of Mortimer, Masques and Entertainments*. Volume 7 of eleven volumes. Oxford: At the Clarendon Press.

HESLOP, T.A. 1987. «English Seals in the Thirteenth and Fourteenth Centuries.» In: ALEXANDER, Jonathan and Paul BINSKI (eds.). 1987. *Age of Chivalry: Art in Plantagenet England 1200-1400*. Royal Academy of Arts London. Catalogue published in association with Weidenfeld and Nicolson. London: Weidenfeld and Nicolson, 114-117.

HOBBITONS. 1996. *J.R.R. Tolkien's Songs from Middle-earth*. Nijmegen: Ar Caras Productions.

JOANNES SARESBERIENSIS. c. 1159. *Metalogicus*. In: MIGNE, J.P. (ed.). 1853. *Patrologiae Latinae*. Vol. 199. Paris. Re-published on CD ROM as *Patrologia Latina Database* by Chadwyck-Haley Inc. 1995.

JÓNSSON, Guðni (ed.). 1954. *Edda Snorra Sturlusonar*. Akureyri: Odds Björnssonar.

LACHEVRE, Frédéric (ed.). 1968. *Les Oeuvres Libertines de Cyrano de Bergerac*. Two volumes. Reprint of the Paris edition 1908-1928 in fifteen volumes. Geneva: Slatkine Reprints.

LANG, Andrew (ed.). 1897. *The Nursery Rhyme Book*. Illustrated by L. Leslie Brooke. London and New York: Frederick Warne & Co.

MACLAREN, A. 1815. *The Man in the Moon: Or, Tumble Down Nap*. A dramatic piece with songs in two acts. London: Printed and sold for the Author by A. Macpherson.

MENNER, Robert J. 1949. «The Man in the Moon and Hedging.» *Journal of English and Germanic Philology (JEGP)* 48:1-14.

MERTON, Robert K. 1965. *On the Shoulders of Giants: A Shandean Postscript*. New York: The Free Press.

MÜLLER-MEININGEN, Johanna. 1984. *Die Morskentänzer und andere Arbeiten des Erasmus Gasser für das Alte Rathaus in München*. Munich and Zurich: Schnell & Steiner.

NICOLSON, Marjorie Hope. 1936. *A World in the Moon: A Study of the Changing Attitude towards the Moon in the Seventeenth and Eighteenth Centuries*. Smith College Studies in Modern Language Series 17.2. Northampton, Mass.: Smith College.

- - -. 1960. *Voyages to the Moon*. 1st edition 1948. New York: Macmillan.

OPIE, Iona and Peter (eds.). 1997. *The Oxford Dictionary of Nursery Rhymes*. 2nd, corrected edition. 1st edition 1951. Oxford: At the Clarendon Press.

OXFORD ENGLISH DICTIONARY (OED). 1989. 2nd edition. Edited by J.A. Simpson and E.S.C. Weiner. Twenty volumes. Oxford: At the Claredon Press.

PHILAGATUS. 1683. *The Informer's Doom: Or, an amazing and seasonable letter from Utopia, directed to the Man in the Moon*. London: Printed for John Dunton.

PITTAWAY, Rev. Thomas. 1934. *The Man in the Moon and Other Lyrics*. Frome: E.L. Bray (Printer).

PRAETORIUS, Johannes. 1666. *Antropodemvs Plvtonicvs. Das ist / Eine Neue Weltbeschreibung von allerley Wunderbahren Menschen*. Magdeburg: In Verlegung Johann Lüderwalds.

R. 1872. *The Man in the Moon and Other Tales*. Glasgow: James Maclehose.

REISS, Edmund. 1963. «Chaucer's Friar and the Man in the Moon.» *Journal of English and Germanic Philology (JEGP)* 62:481-485.

RICKWORD, Edgell (ed.). 1971. *Radical Squibs & Loyal Ripostes*. Satirical Pamphlets of the Regency Period, 1819-1821. Illustrated by George Cruikshank and others. Bath: Adams & Dart.

ROGERS, William Elford. 1972. *Image and Abstraction: Six Middle English Religious Lyrics*. Copenhagen: Rosenkilde and Bagger.

S.S. 1657. *The Man in the Moone Discovering a World of Knavery under the Svnne*. London: Printed for Charles Tyus.

SCULL, Christina and Wayne G. HAMMOND. 1998. «Introduction.» In: TOLKIEN, J.R.R. 1998. *Roverandom*. Edited by Christina Scull and Wayne G. Hammond. London: HarperCollins, ix-xxii.

SEIBERT, Jutta. 1980. *Lexikon christlicher Kunst: Themen, Gestalten, Symbole*. Freiburg i. Br.: Herder.

SHIPPEY, Tom A. 1992. *The Road to Middle Earth*. 2nd revised edition. 1st edition 1982. London: Grafton.

SINGLETON, Charles S. (ed. and trans.). 1970. *Dante Alighieri: The Divine Comedy: Inferno*. Italian text and translation (Part 1) and commentary (Part 2). Bollingen Series LXXX. Princeton, N.J.: Princeton University Press.

- - - (ed. and trans.). 1975. *Dante Alighieri: The Divine Comedy: Paradiso*. Italian text and translation (Part 1) and commentary (Part 2). Bollingen Series LXXX. Princeton, N.J.: Princeton University Press.

STEWARD, Ray M. 1905. *The Surprising Adventures of the Man in the Moon*. Illustrated by L.J. Bridgman. London and Edinburg: T.C. & E.C. Jack.

STOKES, Whitley (ed. and trans.). 1863. *Gwreans an Bys: The Creation of the World*. A Cornish mystery, written by William Jordan 1611. Published for the Philological Society by A. Asher & Co. Berlin: Asher.

THOMPSON, Stith. 1955-58. *Motif-Index of Folk-Literature*. Six volumes. Revised and enlarged edition. Copenhagen: Rosenkilde and Bagger.

THOMSON, W. 1783. *The Man in the Moon; Or, Travels into the Lunar Regions by the Man of the People*. Volume 1. London: Printed for J. Murray.

TOLKIEN, J.R.R. 1968. *The Lord of the Rings*. One-volume edition. Text of the 2nd revised edition of 1966. 1st edition 1954-1955 in three volumes. Reprinted as paperback 1992. London: Grafton.

- - -. 1981. *The Hobbit*. 4th edition. Original edition 1937. London: Unwin Paperbacks.

- - -. 1983. *The Book of Lost Tales: Part I*. Edited by Christopher Tolkien. Volume 1 of The History of Middle-earth. London: George Allen & Unwin.

- - -. 1986. *The Shaping of Middle-earth*. Edited by Christopher Tolkien. Volume 4 of The History of Middle-earth. London: George Allen & Unwin.

- - -. 1988. *The Return of the Shadow*. Edited by Christopher Tolkien. Volume 6 of The History of Middle-earth. London: Unwin Hyman.

- - -. 1989. *The Treason of Isengard*. Edited by Christopher Tolkien. Volume 7 of The History of Middle-earth. London: Unwin Hyman.

- - -. 1994. *The Silmarillion*. Edited by Christopher Tolkien. 1st edition 1977. London: HarperCollins.

- - -. 1995. *The Adventures of Tom Bombadil and Other Verses from The Red Book*. First published by Allen & Unwin 1962. HarperCollins: London.

- - -. 1997. «On Fairy-Stories.» Originally Andrew Lang Lecture given on 8 March 1939, first published in 1947. In: TOLKIEN, J.R.R. 1997. *The Monster and the Critics and Other Essays*. Edited by Christopher Tolkien. London: HarperCollins, 109-161.

- - -. 1998. *Roverandom*. Edited by Christina Scull and Wayne G. Hammond. London: HarperCollins.

- - -. 1999. *Letters from Father Christmas*. Expanded edition. Edited by Baillie Tolkien. London: HarperCollins.

TOYNBEE, Paget. 1906. «'Cain' as a Synonym of the Moon.» *The Athenæum* No. 4104 (June 23, 1906):776.

VAN HELDEN, Albert (ed. and trans.). 1989. *Galileo Galilei: Sidereus Nuncius or The Sidereal Messenger (1610)*. Chicago and London: The University of Chicago Press.

WILDERS, John (ed.). 1967. *Samuel Butler: Hudibras*. Oxford: At the Clarendon Press.

WILKINS, John. 1638. *The Discovery of a World in the Moone. Or, A Discovrse Tending to Prove, that 'tis probable there may be another habitable World in that Planet*. London: Printed by E. G. for Michael Sparl and Edward Forrest.

WRIGHT, Thomas (ed.). 1863. *Alexandri Neckam, De Naturis Rerum Libri Duo*. Rolls Series No. 34. London: Longman, Green, Longman, Roberts and Green.

SECTION 2

BRANCH

Tolkien and His Critics: A Critique

PATRICK CURRY

Summary

My paper addresses the question of why Tolkien's work is simultaneously so enduringly popular with readers and so abhorrent to literary critics. It locates the answer in what I define as modernity, as a project to which the latter are heavily committed but about the former are very worried. Both sets of people are responding (in different ways) to the anti-modernism implicit in Tolkien's creation, which – I argue – has been justified by subsequent events, and in the light of which his book has assumed a new and urgent set of 'postmodern' meanings. I criticize Tolkien's modernist critics (including literary modernist, Marxist, feminist and psychoanalytic variants) in some detail, as well as sketching out those positive meanings.

Introduction

I want to consider the work of J.R.R. Tolkien in terms of its reception, which combines remarkable popular success with extraordinary critical hostility.[1] What are so many readers finding so rewarding in these books that so many professional literary intellectuals think is so bad? The solution to this riddle, I suggest, arises out of the meaning and values of his work as apprehended by both sets of readers, constellated around the idea, values and projects of modernity – something which Tolkien's alternative, 're-enchanted' world fundamentally questions. Crucial too, therefore, are various aspects of what has come to be called postmodernity which, taken together, imply a passing of modernist hegemony. To put it crudely, then, I intend to use postmodernism to defend the contemporary meaning of

---

1 My recent book, Curry (1997), concentrates more on the positive content of Tolkien's work as construed by readers; this paper takes the 'via negativa' of tackling his critics directly. The latter is also written in a somewhat more academic vein. There is, however, some unavoidable overlap.

Tolkien's anti-modernism against his numerous Marxist, materialist, psychoanalytic and structuralist critics. But I shall also use the issue of re-enchantment to criticize postmodernist secularism. I finish up with a few suggestions about both criticism and the writing of fantasy which arise out of this approach.

Without suggesting a comparable importance, a certain parallelism with Tolkien's famous lecture on *Beowulf* has emerged in the course of my own essay, except that this time, the story is contemporary literature, and the irritatingly atavistic and intractable monster at its centre is *The Lord of the Rings* itself. I too am going to suggest that the latter's critics too have missed its point, and have done so for reasons which turn on their own relationship of complicity with modernity. For this purpose, Tolkien's most important text is his profound essay «On Fairy-Stories».

Their doubts are evidently not shared by the reading public. *The Lord of the Rings* (first published in 1954-55) has so far sold about fifty million copies world-wide. This makes it a candidate for the biggest-selling single work of fiction in the twentieth century. *The Hobbit* (1937) stands at about fourty million. And one could add the considerable sales, now perhaps over two million, of his dark and difficult posthumously-published epic *The Silmarillion*. His books have been translated into more than thirty languages, including Japanese, Catalan, Estonian, Greek, Hebrew, Finnish and Indonesian. Furthermore, Tolkien has outlived the 60s counterculture in which he first flourished; as a now unfashionable author, he still sells steadily. In England, for example, since figures began to be kept in 1991, his books have been taken out of public libraries around 200,000 times a year; he is one of only four 'classic authors' whose annual lending totals exceed 300,000 (well ahead of Austen, Dickens and Shakespeare). *The Hobbit* spent fifteen years as the biggest-selling American paperback, and *The Lord of the Rings* has been (and still is) the most valuable first-edition published in this half of the 20th century.[2]

---

2   Relatively conservative estimates, based on figures supplied to me by HarperCollins and by Houghton Mifflin (courtesy Richard McAdoo), and on those in Ezard (1991). *Gone With the Wind* has sold about twenty-seven million copies, and according to the *Guiness Book of Records* of 1991, the single modern novel with the highest global sales is

In other words, we are talking about a massively popular and successful publishing phenomenon, all the more so when one of the books in question is half-a-million words long, and neither involves any money or explicit sex – two ingredients now normally considered essential for bestsellers – let alone cannibalism, sadomasochism, serial murder or lawyers. (And how many of those will even be in print half a century after publication? The fate of Jackie Collins beckons.) Of course, without its sheer unlikeliness – an epic centred on a race of three-and-a-half-foot high creatures and a magic ring, etc. – the success of *The Lord of the Rings* would have much less literary interest; but given that unlikeliness, it should have a great deal.

This popular success was recently confirmed in Britain by the largest survey of readers ever conducted there, sponsored by Waterstone's books and Channel 4 television. Over 26,000 readers were asked to choose the most important books of the century. *The Lord of the Rings* came undisputed first. It was followed in second and third places by Orwell's *1984* and *Animal Farm*. Such a result was not as anomalous as it first appears: both authors, one from a conservative perspective and the other from a socialist, were deeply concerned by the direction of modernity. So too, evidently, are many readers.

As if confirmation was needed, the Waterstone's poll was followed by a survey by the Folio Society of its members (in April 1997), 10,000 of whom voted *The Lord of the Rings* their favourite book. (Interestingly, in a vote about the favourite books of under-sixteen's by 11,000 bookshop customers and viewers of the TV programme *Bookworm*, *The Hobbit* came

---

Jacqueline Susann's *Valley of the Dolls* (1966) – 28,712,000, as of March 1987. (Of course, this may have been subsequently superceded.) Translations: based on information kindly supplied by HarperCollins in 1982. Fashionability: Park (1991). In a recent survey of readers' 'favourite novel' by the *Sunday Times* (24.9.95), with almost 1100 respondents, *The Lord of the Rings* came second (behind *Pride and Prejudice*). A survey of teenagers' reading habits showed *The Lord of the Rings* still high among fifteen to sixteen year-olds (*Guardian*, 16.2.95). Still sells: in England, my assertion can be confirmed by talking to the relevant buyer for any largish book-store. Libraries: Public Lending Right figures: see also *Times Literary Supplement* (14.1.94), and *Guardian* (7.1.93). Value: M. Hime, writing in *Firsts* 5.10 (Oct. 1995):41.

fifth but *The Lord of the Rings* did not figure at all – thus confirming, I think, that it is not essentially a children's book.)[3]

The Critics

Yet this reception has been accompanied by an equally remarkable critical disdain. Primarily, there is silence. A few examples: Margaret Drabble's *Oxford Companion to English Literature* (1985) gives Tolkien exactly thirteen lines out of 1154 pages; Drabble and Stringer's *Oxford Concise Companion to English Literature* (1996; more than 650 pages) has twelve lines; in Saunders's *Short Oxford History of English Literature* (1994; 678 pages) there is no mention at all.[4] I cannot see how this can be described as other than an unconscionable dereliction of duty on the part of people whose profession is supposedly to comprehend literature.

The other principal critical response, which comes no closer to an attempt to understand, has been vitriolic abuse. In Walter Schepp's catalogue (1975:52), Tolkien has been accused of being "paternalistic, reactionary, anti-intellectual, racist, fascistic and, perhaps worst of all in contemporary terms, irrelevant." Goldthwaite's recent book (1996) on "Make-Believe", claiming to be "A Guide to the Principal Works", dismisses *The Lord of the Rings* – the most developed, sustained and influential of such works (even if you don't happen to like it) – as "Faerie-land answer to *Conan the Barbarian*" (Goldthwaite 1996:218). Otherwise good critics don't seem to be able to cope with Tolkien at all, and even his own biographer (Et tu, Brute?) has fatuously opined that "he doesn't really

---

3   These results were carried and discussed by every major British national broadsheet on 20 January 1997. *The Daily Telegraph* apparently repeated the poll, and obtained exactly the same first three places. See also my article in the *New Statesman* of 31 January 1997. Folio Society result: *The Times* and *The Daily Telegraph*, 23 April 1997; Bookworm: *The Guardian*, 1 September 1997.

4   There is at least a reasonable entry in Stringer (1996).

belong to literature or to the arts, but more to the category of people who do things with model railways in their garden sheds."[5]

There are certainly dissenters – Shippey, Elgin, Attebery, Le Guin, Swinfen, Rosebery, Flieger and Filmer to name some – but the high quality of their work must not be confused with its degree of influence in the professional literary, critical and academic world and its publishing outlets. Indeed, in Tolkien's case the two seem inversely related. This goes beyond mere unfashionability; Tolkien's name in such circles is the kiss-of-death.[6] The extreme nature of these responses is thus as fascinating as Tolkien's popular success. Since my book concentrates on the latter, I am mainly concerned here with the critical phenomenon. So let us consider the justice of the charges, and try to determine what lies behind them.

For reasons that will, I hope, become clear, I am going to call the dominant intellectual reaction to Tolkien, and the values that drive it, 'modernism'. There are other possible terms; one, with considerable overlap, is 'humanism'. It is no coincidence that David Ehrenfeld, in his brilliant book on *The Arrogance of Humanism*, is able to read and learn from Tolkien in a way that none of his modernist/humanist critics apparently can. Unlike them, Ehrenfeld does not subscribe to the cult of reason, especially science, accepts the reality and indeed necessity of limits; and prizes what we are fast losing in the current "spectacle of global waste and destruction" (1978:255).

---

5   I have never figured out whether Schepps is being ironic or not; he seems to be saying that the values in Tolkien's work are fine as long as one doesn't try to "apply" them to the so-called real world – a tortuous and unsatisfying conclusion, to say the least. See also West (1970), Johnson (1986), and Hammond (1995). Good critics: e.g., Lurie (1990). Humphrey Carpenter made the last-quoted extraordinary remark on BBC *Bookshelf*, 22.11.1991. See also Raffel (1968:246), who concludes patronizingly that it is "magnificent but [...] not literature."

6   Initially, W.H. Auden and C.S. Lewis; more recently, Shippey (1992), Elgin (1985), Attebery (1992), Le Guin (1989), Swinfen (1984), Rosebery (1992), Flieger (1983), and Filmer (1992). This list is not intended to be exhaustive. For interesting additional comments on Tolkien's rejection by the English literary establishment, see Shippey (1995). (I invite anyone who wants empirical confirmation of my last remark to try to interest a mainstream and/or leading academic publisher in producing a serious book on Tolkien.)

It will be noticed that my examples nearly all fall politically left-of-centre. There are two reasons for this. One is that there seem to be more relevant critics of that political persuasion than right-wing or conservative ones; Tolkien failed the 'PC' test well 'avant la lettre'. The second is that characteristically, the latter have mostly been content to call it a matter of taste and leave it at that. Their general view was perhaps best summed up by the poet John Heath-Stubbs, with that perceptiveness and unfairness required by all the best 'bons mots': "A combination of Wagner and Winnie-the-Pooh."[7] There are thus fewer arguments with which to engage.

Whatever other reasons remain, however, they do not include any right-wing agenda on my part. Indeed, a crucial part of my motivation is the way Tolkien's critics' simple-minded dogmatism actually betrays their own ideals, many of which I share. And I make no apology for writing with some animus. If it were true, as one irenic Tolkien scholar (Timmons 1996:11) believes, that "narrow-minded and hostile views are best countered through sound analyses of the author's works, rather than by bellicose rebuttals", then given such work by the authors just mentioned, the attitude I have been describing would not still hold sway. Of course, my polemic may not succeed either; but that is no reason to refrain from disturbing a cozy and fraudulent orthodoxy.

It is also relevant that another meaning of 'animus' is animating soul or feeling. The ignorant arrogance I am contesting here was never better summed up than by Roz Kaveney (1991), who concluded in an article on Tolkien's centenary that his books are "worth intelligent reading, but not passionate attention." Precisely the opposite conviction drives this paper, and the book (Curry 1997) to which it is a companion piece.

Homage

It was only after much the greater part of this paper had already been written that I discovered its full and proper theoretical context in Barbara Herrnstein

---

7 A remark to the author.

Smith's superlative *Contingencies of Value* (1988).[8] Consider this: Smith (1988:17) dares to point out that "the entire problematic of value and evaluation" – as distinct from that of interpretation – "has been evaded and explicitly exiled by the literary academy." As we shall see in what follows, in the case of Tolkien (and there must be many other possible examples) this ban has allowed an axiologically pathological intellectual culture to flourish, where 'interpretation' is actually driven by a tacit evaluation which cannot be brought out into the open and properly discussed.

Second, Smith (1988:25) calls into question the "claims and judgements of literary value made by or on behalf of what may be called *noncanonical audience*, such as all those readers who are not now students, critics, or professors of literature and perhaps never were and never will be within the academy or on its outskirts." Just such claims and judgements are second nature – indeed, are indispensible – to the shoddy work of Tolkien's critics.

Third, as she writes,

> What is being missed here is that there is a politics of personal *taste* as well as a politics of institutional evaluation and explicit evaluative criticism. This resistance is displayed, moreover, not only by conservative members of the literary academy but also by those who are otherwise most concerned to indicate the political implications of these issues; and the revulsion of academics and intellectuals at the actual literary preferences, forms of aesthetic enjoyment, and general modes of cultural consumption of nonacademics and nonintellectuals – including those whose *political* emancipation they may otherwise seek to promote – has been a familiar feature of the cultural-political scene since at least the 1930s. [...] [O]ppositional cultural theory and conservative humanism have repeatedly generated strictly parellel (and, indeed, often indistinguishable) accounts to explain the tastes of other people in such a way as to justify the academic intellectual's revulsion at them.

(Smith 1988:25-26)

---

8 Nonetheless, obviously, Smith cannot be held to account for my uses of her work.

As unwitting witnesses, I call upon two prominent critics reacting to the news of *The Lord of the Rings* topping the recent Waterstone's survey. Germaine Greer, in W [*Waterstone's Magazine*] (Winter/Spring 1997:4) wrote that "it has been my nightmare that Tolkien would turn out to be the most influential writer of the twenieth century. The bad dream has materialized." And Auberon Waugh, in *The Times* (20.1.97), described the result as "suspicious", and suggested that Tolkien's fans may have orchestrated a campaign. (To quote Helen Armstrong, in *The Guardian* (23.1.97), of the Tolkien Society – membership: approximately 500 – "In our dreams!") As an apodictically perfect demonstration of "Marxist cultural critics join[ing] Arnoldian humanists in deploring the novel/alien cultural productions of the late twentieth century" (Smith 1988:75), this would take some beating!

Infantile?

The critical rubbishing of Tolkien began with Edmund Wilson's extended sneer (1956:312) about "juvenile trash" in 1956. Younger readers today may need reminding that Wilson was a pathologically ambitious critic who championed modernism in literature (and Stalinism in politics).[9] In his pompous obsession, as a contemporary put it, "with being the Adult in the room" (Parker 1956-57:608) – and maybe, oddly enough, his priapism too – Wilson is a good exemplar of what Ursula Le Guin (1989:125-26) called "a deep puritanical distrust of fantasy" on the part of those who "confuse fantasy, which in the psychological sense is a universal and essential faculty of the human mind, with infantilism and pathological regression."

Le Guin is undoubtedly right about Wilson and others of his ilk, but in a demonstration of the durability and ubiquity of this accusation, Tolkien's "infantilism" (along with "nostalgia", to which we shall return later) was recently revived by Michael Moorcock (1987). Perhaps, therefore, it is no coincidence that Moorcock has now mostly abandoned his science fiction/fantasy – part of whose real appeal was precisely their rather

---

9 See Meyers (1995).

adolescent charm ('my, what a long sword you have!') – to write supposedly Adult novels. In any case, many science fiction writers are indeed committed modernists; and not a few are poorly placed to finger infantilism – witness in both respects, for example, the toys-for-boys technological fetishism of J.G. Ballard.

As Tolkien («On Fairy-Stories», 1988:43) noted, the connection between children and fairy-stories is an accident of history, not something essential: "If a fairy-story as a kind is worth reading at all it is worthy to be written for and read by adults." But being Grown-Up is a recurring theme in modernism, with its teleological fantasy of collectively progressing towards the truth, and its mythoclasm as a necessary destructiveness in order to get there. *The Lord of the Rings* and its readers are thus doubly stigmatized, both individually/psychologically and collectively/socially. Tolkien's enormous popularity then requires such risible explanations as Robert Giddings's (1981) "PR men", at whose behest the reading public apparently took him up solely because it was told to do so.

It is true, however, that modernist hostility to Tolkien need not be of the left. *Private Eye* sneered that Tolkien appeals only to those "with the mental age of a child – computer programmers, hippies and most Americans" (see Craig 1992). And despite his trumpeted sensitivity to elite literary contempt for the reading public, the populist Oxford professor John Carey (1977:631) repeated the charge of childishness, and attacked Tolkien for his lack of interest in "the writers who were moulding English literature in his own day – Eliot, Joyce, Lawrence" – as if English literature, to quote Brian Rosebury (1992:133), were "a single substance, appropriated for a definite period, like the only blob of Plasticene in the classroom, by an exclusive group (however gifted) [...]."

Useful to Get That Learned

Catherine Stimpson raised several frequent objections in 1969; they are worth noting symptomatically as having successfully set the tone for much subsequent Tolkien criticism. "An incorrigible nationalist," she wrote of Tolkien, his epic "celebrates the English bourgeois pastoral idyll. Its characters, tranquil and well fed, live best in placid, philistine, provincial rural cosiness." Second, his characters are one-dimensional, dividing neatly into "good & evil, nice & nasty" (Stimpson 1969:8). (She was preceded in this criticism, repeatedly, by Edwin Muir, in 1954-55.) Third, Tolkien's language reveals "class snobbery". Finally, Stimpson (1969:13) writes:

> Behind the moral structure is a regressive emotional pattern. For Tolkien is irritatingly, blandly, traditionally masculine. [...] He makes his women characters, no matter what their rank, the most hackneyed of stereotypes. They are either beautiful and distant, simply distant, or simply simple.[10]

Taking these points in order, one could reply to the first that the hobbits (excepting Bilbo and Frodo, and perhaps Sam; well, and Merry and Pippin) would indeed have preferred to live quiet rural lives – if they could have. Unfortunately for them, and her point, there is much more to Middle-earth than the Shire. By the same token, any degree of English nationalism that the hobbits represent is highly qualified. Tolkien himself pointed out that

> hobbits are not a Utopian vision, or recommended as an ideal in their own or any age. They, as all peoples and their situations, are an historical accident – as the Elves point out to Frodo – and an impermanent one in the long view.
>
> (*Letters* 1981:197)

It is also possible, as Jonathan Bate (1991) suggests, to draw a distinction between love of the land and love of the fatherland; and in *The Lord of the Rings*, the lovingly detailed specificities of its natural world – which include but far outrun those of the Shire – far exceed the latter. But I shall return to these questions below.

As for one-dimensional, good/bad characters, Stimpson has either ignored or missed the inner struggles, with widely varying results, of Frodo, Gollum, Boromir, and Denethor. As Le Guin again has noted, several major characters have a 'shadow', and in Frodo's case, there are arguably two: Sam, and Gollum – who is himself doubled as Gollum/Stinker and Smeagol/Slinker, as Sam calls them. And each race – with the exception of

---

10 See Colebatch's (1990:61-66) critique of Stimpson.

orcs, and even they violently differed with each other – is a collection of good, bad and indifferent individuals. Le Guin (1989:57-8) asks, "When you look at it that way, can you call it a simple story? I suppose so. *Oedipus Rex* is a fairly simple story, too. But it is not simplistic."[11]

Regarding class snobbery: in *The Hobbit*, perhaps; the book's other virtues (such as its quality as a story), and its having been written more than half a century ago, will hardly put off zealous contemporary detectors of orcism and trollism. But with *The Lord of the Rings*, this charge does not stand up. There is certainly class awareness; but orc speech is not all the same: there are at least three kinds, and none are necessarily "working-class" (see Rosebury 1992:75-76), while the idioms of the various hobbits only correspond to their social classes in the same way as do those of contemporary humans (see Johannesson 1997). Furthermore, the accent and idiom of Sam (arguably the real hero of the book) and most other hobbits is that of a rural peasantry; while those of virtually all of Tolkien's major villains – Smaug, Saruman, the Lord of the Nazgûl (and presumably Sauron too) – are unmistakably posh. There is also the blindingly obvious fact of *The Lord of the Rings* as a tale of "the hour of the Shire-folk, when they arise from their quiet fields to shake the towers and counsels of the Great." (*LotR* 1991:I, 354)[12]. Like many of Stimpson's accusations, however, that of pandering to social hierarchy has proved durable.[13] But as will become increasingly apparent, card-carrying modernists find it almost impossible to bring themselves actually to *read* Tolkien.

Sexist?

Then there is the question of Tolkien's, or rather, Middle-earth's, masculinity. How irritating it is will vary wildly with individual readers

---

11 Cf. Attebery (1992:33) and Rosebury (1992:75-76).
12 All references are to the three-volume edition of 1991.
13 For a recent repetition, see Kavaney (1991) who also associates Tolkien with "a broadside attack on modernism and even realism" (is *nothing* sacred?), and anachronistically blames him for current "American commercial fantasy and science fiction".

(including women); but in this case it is tempting to reply, guilty as charged. As evidence to the contrary, there are the characters of Galadriel and Éowyn, without whom *The Lord of the Rings* would be seriously impoverished, and who are more complex and conflicted than Stimpson allows. Galadriel in particular is a powerful and wise woman who dominates her somewhat obtuse spouse, and refuses the Ring out of strength rather than fear or weakness (see Ewijck 1995). Still, Tolkien's paternalism is unmistakable, and *The Lord of the Rings* is indeed a male-centred text. (Incidentally, he (*Letters* 1981:293) described the family arrangements of hobbits as "'patrilinear' rather than patriarchal. [...] [M]aster and mistress had equal status, if different functions.")

Yet Tolkien has arguably committed no crime worse than being a man of his time and place, or failing to transcend it in the way J.S. Mill, say, did his in relation to feminist issues. And it is too easy to ask a work to be something it isn't, or its author to do something he or she didn't set out to do. Indeed, maybe we should be grateful that Tolkien didn't attempt a more feminine Middle-earth. Without prejudice to those male writers who have succeeded in placing believable female characters at the centre of their work, the results can be ghastly.[14] Imagine what Tolkien might have wrought!

Perhaps we should also be glad that academic and literary feminists have largely ignored Tolkien (presumably as beyond the pale), and thus spared him the fate of, say, Willa Cather. Cather's plain lack of interest in sex and gender, and the focus in her fiction on quite other matters, has not prevented the kind of gross reductionism whereby "No tree can grow, no river flow in Cather's landscapes without its being a penis or a menstrual period" (Acacella 1995:70). I say "largely" because one essay has already shown what would be the result: Tolkien and Lewis (both devoted husbands) driven by repressed homosexuality, swords all phalli, Shelob a metaphor for female genitalia and Tolkien's fear of female sexuality, and

---

14 I am thinking of two otherwise excellent writers, John Fowles and Dennis Potter, in *The Mantissa* and *Blackeyes* respectively.

even the phial of Galadriel – one of his book's several heroines – somehow, a super-phallus (Partridge 1983).

Notwithstanding such silliness, however, I think the male centredness of Tolkien's work should be acknowledged as a real limitation. But it is undeniable that countless women have enjoyed and even loved *The Lord of the Rings*. It would be the height of arrogance to accuse them all of gender-false-consciousness. I think the reason is simply that no sane and intelligent reader allows any single issue, including gender, to completely dominate all other considerations; so intelligent/non-dogmatic women, including feminists, are getting the other things from Tolkien that are so richly present, and some of which, such as reverence for nature, arguably relate to ecofeminism. I would also point out that to insist on such a dominance presumes to dictate what women's consciousness (and, by implication, men's) can and cannot experience and participate in; in its implicit 'realism', it is thus also a particularly inappropriate demand in relation to *fantasy* literature, of all things.[15]

Incidentally, a related charge is the lack of sex – or rather, since there is a good deal of progenitivity, a lack of explicit or erotic sex. (Norman Talbot once remarked, with some justice, that the most erotic character in *The Lord of the Rings* is Shelob.) In a curious and historically very recent inversion of puritanism, this absence seems to present some readers with real difficulties. Thus, Kenneth MacLeish (1983:27) says that its absence is a serious problem for those who claim a higher status for *The Lord of the Rings* than that of a "simple tale". In addition to making unnecessary concessions to the fetish of a Canon, this is surely ridiculous: is *Moby Dick* therefore a simple tale, or *A Portrait of the Artist as a Young Man*?

Racist?

Another unpleasant accusation sometimes made, related perhaps to that of class snobbery, is racism. It is true that Tolkien's (*LotR* 1991:II, 14, 357) evil creatures are frequently "swart, slant-eyed", and tend to come from the

---

15 I am indebted to Carolyn Burdett for discussion of this point.

south ("the cruel Haradrim") and east ("the wild Easterlings") – both threatening directions in what Schepps (1975:44-45) called Tolkien's "moral cartography". It is also true that black – as in Breath, Riders, Hand, Years, Land, Speech – is often a terrible colour, especially when contrasted with Gandalf the White, the White Rider, and so on. But the primary association of black here is with night and darkness, not race. And there are counter-examples: Saruman's sign is a white hand, Aragorn's standard is mostly black, the Black Riders were not actually black, except their outer robes, and the Black Stone of Erech is connected with Isildur (see Rosebury 1992:79). Rather strikingly, it also seems to have escaped the attention of Tolkien's critics on this point that as far as one can tell, hobbits were not white-skinned but brown (*LotR* 1991:III, 229).

Overall, it is true, Tolkien is drawing on centuries of such moral valuation, not unrelated to historical experience attached to his chosen setting – enemies, in N.W. Europe, have overwhelmingly come from the East – in order to convey something immediately recognisable in the context of his story. As Kathleen Herbert (1993:271) noticed, orcs sound very like the first horrified reports in Europe of the invading Huns of the fourth and fifth centuries: "broad-shouldered, bow-legged, devilishly effective fighters, moving fast, talking a language that sounds like no human speech (probably Turkic) and practising ghastly tortures with great relish."

Perhaps the worst you could say is that Tolkien makes no attempt to forestall the possibility of a racist interpretation. (I say "possibility" because it is ridiculous to assume that readers automatically transfer their feelings about orcs to all the swart or slant-eyed people they encounter in the street.) But as Brian Attebery (1992:33) points out, "this ethical division is rendered increasingly invalid as the story progresses, as evil emerges among the kingly Gondorians, the blond Riders of Rohan, the seemingly incorruptible wizards, and even the thoroughly English hobbit-folk of the Shire." Furthermore, as the anthropologist Virginia Luling (1995:56) has noted, the appearance of racism is deceptive, "not only because Tolkien in his non-fictional writing several times repudiated racist ideas, but because [...] in his sub-creation the whole intellectual underpinning of racism is absent."[16]

Tolkien once wrote:

> In any case if you want to write a tale of this sort you must consult your roots, and a man of the North-West of the Old World will set his heart and the action of his tale in an imaginary world of that air, and that situation: with the Shoreless Sea of his innumerable ancestors to the West, and the endless lands (out of which enemies mostly come) to the East.

(*Letters* 1981:212).

Thus, as Clyde Kilby (1977:51-52) recounts, when Tolkien was asked what lay east and south of Middle-earth, he replied: "'Rhûn is the Elvish word for East. Asia, China, Japan, and all the things which people in the West regard as far away. And south of Harad is Africa, the hot countries.' Then Mr. Resnick asked, 'That makes Middle-earth Europe, doesn't it?' To which Tolkien replied, 'Yes, of course – Northwestern Europe [...] where my imagination comes from.'" (In which case, as Tolkien also indicated, Mordor "'would be roughly in the Balkans.'")

He reacted sharply to reading a description of Middle-earth as 'Nordic', however:

> Not *Nordic*, please! A word I personally dislike; it is associated, though of French origin, with racialist theories. [...] Auden has asserted that for me 'the North is a sacred direction'. That is not true. The North-west of Europe, where I (and most of my ancestors) have lived, has my affection, as a man's home should. I love its atmosphere, and know more of its histories and languages than I do of other parts; but it is not 'sacred', nor does it exhaust my affections.

(*Letters* 1981:375-76)

It is also noticeable that the races in Middle-earth are most striking in their variety and autonomy. Without suggesting that a clear-cut choice exists, but

---

16 However, as Luling (1995:56) adds, the Orcs – as distinct from the Haradrim, Variags and Easterlings – "are a separate problem, and one that Tolkien himself never really solved".

rather as an example of the complexity and ambiguity of his literary myth, is this an instance of ethnocentrism, or multiculturalism? Or even – given that most of the races are closely tied to a particular geography and ecology, and manage to live there without exploiting it to the point of destruction – bioregionalism? Again, one of the subplots of *The Lord of the Rings* concerns an enduring friendship between members of races traditionally estranged (Gimli and Legolas); and the most important wedding in the book, between Aragorn and Arwen, is an interracial marriage. As usual, the picture is a great deal more complex than the critics (although not necessarily the public) seem to see.

The Marxist

A major stream of adverse Tolkien criticism can be traced back to Raymond Williams, who, in *The Country and the City* (1985), noted the

> extraordinary development of country-based fantasy, from Barrie and Kenneth Grahame through J.C. Powys and T.H. White and now to Tolkien. [...] It is then not only that the real land and its people were falsified; a traditional and surviving rural England was scribbled over and almost hidden from sight by what is really a suburban and half-educated scrawl.
> (Williams 1985:258)

Williams has been a massively influential critic.[17] One could produce many other commentators he has influenced: John Lucas (1990:118), for example: "This is the ultimate, deeply conservative, ambition of pastoral. It falsifies the actual relations of non-city communities just as much and for the same reason that it falsifies city communities." And almost interchangeably, Barrell and Bull (1974:5, 8): "The Pastoral allows for a direct opposition to social change, a reactionary clinging to a static present, and an often desperate belief in future improvement." And it fades away with "the

---

17 See O'Connor (1989; especially 109-15). Two disclaimers: I note and appreciate Williams's opening-out of critical vistas from the confines of Leavisism. And I do not mean to subsume Marxism in the work of Williams; there are others, especially Adorno and Horkheimer of the Frankfurt School, who have been deeply sceptical about Enlightenment rationalism.

possibility of social mobility and of economic progress". (How dated this now sounds, as we face increasingly insurmountable problems as a direct result of "economic progress"!)

Let us try to put 'cultural materialism' to work in relation to Tolkien. Williams writes:

> In Britain, identifiably, there is a precarious but persistent rural-intellectual radicalism: genuinely and actively hostile to industrialism and capitalism; opposed to commercialism and the exploitation of the environment; attached to country ways and feelings, the literature and the lore.

(Williams 1985:36-37)

This sounds generous, until you get to the punch-line: "in every kind of radicalism the moment comes when any critique must choose its bearings, between past and future [...]." Furthermore, "We must begin differently: not in the idealisations of one order or another, but in the history to which they are only partial and misleading responses." By the same token, in our current crises myth and revolution must be seen as "alternative", not complementary responses. In other words, we must have "real history" oriented to a revolutionary future, not "myth" dreaming of the past (Williams 1985:247).

But this set of shibboleths (itself profoundly mythical in character) entails a false set of choices – the mythical *vs.* the actual, the ideal *vs.* the real – that are as politically damaging as they are philosophically naive. It conflates materialism with matter and idealism with ideas, thus missing the crucial and highly 'material' effects of the latter. It is essentialist in holding the political character of traditions and positions to be inherent and fixed. And it ignores the massive lesson that the Left, within Williams's lifetime, should have learned from Mrs Thatcher if not Gramsci: that people do not live by factual and historical bread alone, but also by ideas, values and visions of alternatives.[18] In other words, we are looking at something that includes but goes well beyond Williams's moral "self-righteousness", "a

---

18 To be fair, this is something that the best of Williams's former students, such as Stuart Hall, absorbed and have themselves said.

basically utilitarian attitude to art", "the claggy dreariness of his writing", and "a terrible puritanism at the heart of the criticism written by those who still follow Williams", as Tom Paulin, in *The Independent on Sunday* (16.4.95), argues.[19] These problems are *structural*.[20]

Nostalgic?

Perhaps it is not surprising, then, that Williams's treatment of pastoralism terminates in mere abuse of Tolkien's work as, absurdly, "half-educated" and "suburban". (Tolkien (*Letters* 1981:65) actually complained to his son in 1943 that "the bigger things get the smaller and duller or flatter the globe gets. It is getting to be all one blasted little provincial suburb.")

Nor has Williams noticed that the hobbits' pastoralism is dominated and subverted by other themes. As Gildor said to Frodo, "it is not your own Shire. [...] Other dwelt here before hobbits were; and others will dwell here when hobbits are no more. The wide world is all about you: you can fence yourselves in, but you cannot for ever fence it out." And as Merry too admitted, "It is best to love first what you are fitted to love, I suppose: you must start somewhere and have some roots, and the soil of the Shire is deep. Still there are some things deeper and higher; and not a gaffer could tend his garden in what he calls peace but for them, whether he knows about them or not" (*LotR* 1991:I, 120; III, 174). *The Lord of the Rings* could thus properly be seen as an extended argument that pastoralism as such is *not* enough – doomed, even: "The Shire is not a haven, and the burden of the tale is that there are no havens in a world where evil is a reality. If you think you live in

---

19 A good example is Williams's ex-student Terry Eagleton, who eulogized him as author of "the most profound and original collection of cultural writing in 20th-century Britain" (*New Statesman & Society*, 13.10.95). As late as 1994, Eagleton was still touchingly defining culture as "a transitional point between religion and politics" («Discourse & Discos», *Times Literary Supplement*, 15.7.94).

20 See Felperin (1985:206-07): "The marxist fideo-materialism, with its fundamentalist ground of History and utopian goal of socialism to support and guide its reading of texts, is rather a dogmatism, another secular theology in which the old transcendental signifieds of God and the Bourgeois Author may have been superseded or sublated by History but certainly not dispensed with."

one, you are probably naive like the early Frodo, and certainly vulnerable" (Grant 1981:99).

Perhaps the political problem is the richness and centrality of the natural world in Middle-earth (and not just pastoral nature). But if so, it only serves to confirm that the Left, qua Williams & Co., remains stuck in a modernist, economistic and incipiently Stalinist problematic. Had it accepted William Morris's generous offer to meet halfway, in E.P. Thompson's terms, this tragedy need never have happened. But the more recent examples too, of its best representatives, continue to be ignored: Thompson himself, for example – Morris's biographer, a passionate critic of economistic and class reductionism, defender of Blake's counter-hegemonic cultural 'mythos', and not so coincidentally, perhaps, a passionate gardener.[21] And again, Orwell (another gardener), in «Some Thoughts on the Common Toad» (1946):

> Is it wicked to take a pleasure in spring? [...] is it politically reprehensible, while we are all groaning, or at any rate ought to be groaning, under the shackles of the capitalist system, to point out that life is frequently more worth living because of a blackbird's song, a yellow elm tree in October, or some other natural phenomenon which does not cost money and does not have what the editors of left-wing newspapers call a class angle?
> (Ehrenfeld 1993:25)

Orwell and Thompson – along with Dennis Potter – are also distinctive in being at once on the Left and willing to recognize the power and validity of patriotism (as distinct from nationalism), including a specifically English kind. Unfortunately, most of the Left remains terrified of this whole area, thus continuing to cede it to potential political manipulation by the Right of the kind which Mrs Thatcher and Reagan initiated.[22] But for our purposes

---

21 Thompson (1976) and (1993). For Thompson's impressive catalogue of his garden on his 50th birthday, see the *New Left Review* 102 (Sept/Oct 1993).

22 Hence the furious reaction to historian Samuel (1995), who dares to question this shibboleth; typical was that of the nostalgia- and patriotism-phobic Patrick Wright. As a hopeful sign to the contrary, albeit well outside mainstream political (and musical) discourse, note the success in the UK of critically patriotic 'new folk' bands like The Levellers.

here, while rejecting the knee-jerk modernist hostility to this work, note the implied intimacy of nature, 'nostalgia' and place. Together with myth, these are indeed crucially related – something that Tolkien recognized, and *The Lord of the Rings* embodies.

Even in the realm of power (narrowly construed) and its effects, cultural materialism falls down. Fraser Harrison goes straight to the heart of the matter:

> While it is easy to scoff at the whimsicality and commercialism of rural nostalgia, it is also vital to acknowledge that this reaching-out to the countryside is an expression, however distorted, of a healthy desire to find some sense of meaning and relief in a world that seems increasingly bent on mindless annihilation.
>
> (Harrison 1984:170)

Accordingly, says Harrison in a wonderful phrase, "it becomes meaningful to talk of 'radical nostalgia'." Echoing Williams, he agrees that "nostalgia recognizes no duty to history"; he asks us to recognize, however, that

> there is another dimension to nostalgia and that it should not be dismissed as simply a self-indulgent, escapist and pernicious failing. Whereas its account of history is patently untrue, and more ideological than it would pretend, it does none the less express a truth of its own, which reflects an authentic and deeply felt emotion. [...] Our addiction to it is surely a symptom of our failure to make a satisfactory mode of life in the present, but perhaps it can also be seen as evidence of our desire to repair and revitalise our broken relations. The pastoral fantasy nostalgia invented is after all an image of a world in which men and women feel at home with themselves, with each other and with nature, a world in which harmony reigns. It is an ideal [...].
>
> (Harrison 1984:170-71)[23]

Now Tolkien gives us to understand, as strongly as possible while still writing a story and not a tract, that nostalgia pure-and-simple will not

---

23 Cf. Harrison (1992:156): "nostalgia keeps open the vision of historical alternatives [...]."

suffice. In Middle-earth, it is the Elves whose nostalgia is the strongest – both in the sense of yearning for the past and attempting to maintain that past now, in places like Lothlórien and Rivendell. But the Elves, despite their valiant resistance, plainly offer no real solution to the central problem of the Ring. Yet it is also true that his work is suffused with the "pastoral fantasy" of a better world, equally memory and longing, to which Harrison refers. And such ideals have real power in the world.

The 'Problem' of Evil

Tolkien has often been savaged on this question. Thus, Robert Giddings:

> The evil in the world as portrayed by Tolkien has nothing whatever to do with social or economic causes. It is evil, pure and simple. Consequently there is no need for change of socio-economic conditions, the environmental conditions of life, relations between different classes, etc., etc. – all these things which make up the very fabric of a society, *any* society, are perceived by Tolkien as totally beyond any need or possibility of change.
> (Giddings 1983:12-13)[24]

Giddings exaggerates inexcusably – *The Lord of the Rings* is full of 'social, economic and environmental' changes which are not exactly randomly related to the War of the Ring, and the crucial effects of which are recognised by all its participants.

In a related point, I'm really not sure what Nick Otty (1983) means (although it's clearly not meant kindly) when he writes that in *The Lord of the Rings* "There are no concrete or operational assertions which make it clear why we should eschew evil." Is it any less clear why in Middle-earth Mordor should be eschewed than, say, fascism now? Or is he so disabled by a perceived absence of "concrete or operational" instructions and labels that without them he is ready to snuggle up to the first Nazgûl, or contemporary equivalent, that he meets?

---

24 Cf. the similar point made by Jackson (1988:154-55).

However, Giddings is not altogether wrong about Tolkien's position. His characters spend a great deal of their lives, and sometimes lose their lives, combatting evil as it exists in their world. They are therefore active, not quietist, and to that extent not 'escapist'. Nevertheless, as Gandalf repeatedly stresses, that is *all* one can do:

> it is not our part to master all the tides of the world, but to do what is in us for the succour of those years wherein we are set, uprooting the evil in the fields that we know, so that those who live after may have clean earth to till. What weather they shall have is not ours to rule.
>
> (*LotR* 1991:III, 185)

There is no permanent solution. Ultimately, Tolkien is of the same opinion as Primo Levi (1987:188): evil "spreads like a contagion. It is foolish to think that human justice can eradicate it. It is an inexhaustible fount of evil [...]." Or, only slightly less darkly, William Empson (1979:4-5): "it is only in degree that any improvement of society could prevent wastage of human powers; the waste even in a fortunate life, the isolation even in a life rich in intimacy, cannot but be felt deeply, and is the crucial feeling of tragedy." Le Guin (1989:100), not for the first time, puts her finger on it: "Those who fault Tolkien on the Problem of Evil are usually those who have an *answer* to the Problem of Evil – which he did not."

Of course, this issue is itself not the sort of question that comes with an answer in the back of the book, against which yours is 'right' or 'wrong'. While any response to evil is inevitably problematic and incomplete, however, Tolkien's is at least as complex and tenable as that of his more meliorist opponents. And within that problematic, his characters are as activist as anyone could ask, moved by the same kind of ideals that I have just suggested have real power in the primary world. Once again, this is something Tolkien's readers have noticed where his critics have been blind.

Quietist?

To pick a local and contemporary example, there are (mainly) young people trying, as I write, to defend the remaining countryside outside Newbury,

Berkshire, against yet another destructive, expensive and futile bypass. Their principal means of resistance is to put themselves, with extraordinary determination and valour as well as good humour, up trees and literally in the way of an army of security guards, bailiffs, contractors and police, not to mention bulldozers and chainsaws. And among them, I found one person out of dozens who hadn't just read *The Lord of the Rings* but knew it, so to speak, inside out. (Indeed, among its leaders, if that is the word I want, is one Balin.) It is no coincidence, then, that an early supporter of one such proposed bypass, running through Dartmoor, called his opponents "Middle-earth hobbits" (Veldman 1994:110). Nor, for that matter that the fashionable and supposedly avant-garde writer J.G. Ballard dismisses road protesters as a "a group of weirdos that are anti-car".[25] Once again, we must ask, who are really the fantasists, the indulgers in nostalgia, the reactionaries here: Tolkien and his readers, or his modernist critics?

This is not the only example. Once I started looking, having seen through the lie that Tolkien's books are a bucolic retreat from 'reality' that induce an apolitical passivity and/or right-wing quietism, others quickly appeared. Like Meredith Veldman, I too found profound common ground between the work of the left-wing historian and peace activist E.P. Thompson and that of Tolkien. What Veldman calls "the romantic protest movement" unites the CND/END campaign of resistance to nuclear weapons, the ecology movement beginning in the 1970s, and what Veldman calls "Middle-earth as moral protest". Thus, the countercultural success of this otherwise unlikely figure among 60s radicals and dissidents was no anomaly; far from it. In 1972, David Taggart sailed into the French nuclear testing area – an action which led directly to the founding of Greenpeace. His journal records that "I had been reading *The Lord of the Rings*. I could not avoid thinking of parallels between our own little fellowship and the long journey of the hobbits into the volcano-haunted land of Mordor [...]" (Veldman 1994:108). Nor had it escaped Taggart's notice, or Tolkien's other readers unblinded by modernist promises, that Mordor's landscape is one of industrial desolation, polluted beyond renewal; and that such

---

25 Quoted by John Ryle, *Guardian* (25.11.96).

desecration is inseparable from its autocratic, unaccountable and unrestrained exercise of political power.

There seems no reason to shrink from adding that in addition to my having delighted in Tolkien in 1967, the late E.P. Thompson is one of my intellectual and moral exemplars, and I was an active Greenpeace supporter from the mid-1980s; and I still see no contradiction in this combination. But there is no autobiographical element to my final and most recent example. Here is Maria Kamenkovich on Tolkien in the former USSR, where *The Lord of the Rings* circulated in 'samizdat' form:

> Western readers must understand that for us Tolkien was never any kind of 'escape'. When hobbits laughed at the absurd 'distribution', we didn't laugh at all, because the same thing caused millions of deaths among the peasants in the USSR in the 1920s. When Aragorn held up the elf-stone at the parting with the hobbits, we felt desperate because we did not have any hope of winning our battle at home [...].

(Kamenkovich 1992:36)

Thus the Siege of the White House in Moscow found itself intertwined with the Battle of the Green Fields in the Shire:

> Western friends of Russia know what happened in Moscow on 19-22 of August 1991, but I doubt that they were informed that many people remembered Tolkien when they made barricades from trolley-buses (just like hobbits from country wains!). It is important to remember that the first [complete] translation officially published went on sale only a few days before. Moscow members of the Tolkien Society spent all those fearful thunderstorm and rainy nights near the White House holding a defence. The war-machines got as crazy as Oliphants and stamped down three young archers. And Gandalf stood before the King of Angmar saying: 'You shall not pass' [...]

> Tolkien never meant to describe any real events either in the past or the future. But he certainly *added* something to earthy events. It just cannot be helped.[26]
> (Kamenkovich 1992:38)

Maybe our political problem is not too much fantasy, but *not enough of the right kind*.

Fascist?

Raymond Williams says that

> [nostalgic] celebrations of a feudal or aristocratic order [embody values that] spring to the defence of certain kinds of order, certain social hierarchies and moral stabilities, which have a feudal ring but a more relevant and more dangerous contemporary application [...] in the defence of traditional property settlements, or in the offensive against democracy in the name of blood and soil.
> (Williams 1985:35-36)

In the light of the unpleasant implications in the last passage, perhaps this is the place to consider the politics (in the narrow sense) of both Tolkien and Middle-earth. Tolkien noted in 1943 that

> My political opinions lean more and more to Anarchy (philosophically understood, meaning abolition of control not whiskered men with bombs) – or to 'unconstitutional' Monarchy. I would arrest anyone who uses the word State (in any sense other than the inanimate realm of England and its inhabitants, a thing that has neither power, rights nor mind) [...].
> (*Letters* 1981:63)

Actually, arguably anticipating the eco-sabotage of Earth First!, his approval stretched to the war-time "dynamiting [of] factories and power-

---

26 See also Grushetskiy (1995) and Grigorieva (1995); and «Tolkien Fantasies Strike Russian Chord», *The Globe and Mail* (28.5.94).

stations; I hope that, encouraged now as 'patriotism', may remain a habit! But it won't do any good if it is not universal" (*Letters* 1981:63).

Some years later, Tolkien wrote:

> I am not a 'socialist' in any sense – being averse to 'planning' (as must be plain) most of all because the 'planners', when they acquire power, become so bad – but I would not say that we had to suffer the malice of Sharkey and his Ruffians here. Though the spirit of 'Isengard', if not of Mordor, is of course always cropping up. The present design of destroying Oxford in order to accomodate motor-cars is a case. But our chief adversary is a member of a 'Tory' Government.
>
> (*Letters* 1981:235)

He was referring to a narrowly-defeated proposal in 1956 to put a so-called relief road through Christ Church meadow – something with a typically contemporary ring.

So Tolkien himself can be classed as an anarchist (or libertarian) and/or a conservative – not at all in the contemporary sense of the last, which has been almost entirely arrogated by neo-liberalism, but in the sense of striving to conserve what is worth saving. Neither category can easily be assimilated to either Left or Right, which is itself usually sufficient cause to be dismissed by those who like to have these things cut-and-dried. In a consistently pre-modern way, Tolkien was neither liberal nor socialist, nor even necessarily democrat; but neither is there even a whiff of 'blood and soil' fascism.[27] In this, he contrasts strongly with modernists such as T.S. Eliot, Ezra Pound, D.H. Lawrence, Wyndham Lewis and arguably Philip Larkin:[28] writers to whom Tolkien is sometimes unfavourably compared. But his absence from these ranks is no surprise; he was trying to do something completely different. Consider too that besides imperialistic nationalism, of which Tolkien was very suspicious, something common to

---

27 For a fuller discussion of Tolkien's opposition to fascism, see Plank (1975) and Yates (1995).

28 See Harrison (1966); on Larkin, see Hitchens (1993:161-74). W.B. Yeats would appear to be ambiguous here.

all strands of fascism (but especially Nazism) is the worship of technological modernism, which he positively hated.[29]

That antipathy is obvious throughout his works, down to the background detail of, say, the fall of Númenor (Tolkien's Atlantis) through *'hubris'*, which consisted of both domestic political autocracy and intolerance of dissent and a foreign policy based on technological and military supremacy. Actually, German Nazism was a particular tragedy for Tolkien. In 1941, he wrote to his son Michael that

> I have in this War a burning private grudge [against Hitler, for] ruining, perverting, misapplying and making for ever accursed, that noble Northern spirit, a supreme contribution to Europe, which I have ever loved, and tried to present in its true light.
> (*Letters* 1981:55-56)

It is also noteworthy that when the German publishers of *The Hobbit* wrote to Tolkien in 1938 asking if he was of "arisch" (aryan) origins, and could prove it, he refused to do so, indignantly remarking that "if I am to understand that you are enquiring whether I am of *Jewish* origin, I can only reply that I regret that I appear to have *no* ancestors of that gifted people" (*Letters* 1981:37). He consequently advised Allen & Unwin to "let a German translation go hang" (*Letters* 1981:37). It may be, as Tom Paulin has suggested (instancing T.S. Eliot), that anti-Semitism is historically integral to the formation of Englishness; but not in Tolkien's case.

It is true that Tolkien had been shocked by the violent anti-clericalism of the republicans in the Spanish civil war, and for that reason favoured the nationalists; the link here with his Catholicism is direct.[30] But however reactionary and repressive Franco's regime (which I do not dispute), there is no justification for conflating his reactionary conservatism with fascism; and Spain was noticeable in the Second World War, despite intense pressure from Hitler, by its neutrality.

Nor is Middle-earth fascist, let alone Nazi. The Shire, for example, functions by a sort of municipal (not representative) democracy, which

---

29 See Bauman (1989), Payne (1996), and Herf (1984).
30 See Tolkien (1981:95-96).

Tolkien himself described as "half republic half aristocracy" (*Letters* 1981:241). The former half has, typically, been ignored by Tolkien's critics in their eagerness to assail the latter; but even here, their case is weak. Of the three positions of authority in the Shire, two are hereditary and one elected; but their powers (and duties) are minimal. True, by the end of *The Lord of the Rings* there is again a King; but he merely grants to the Shire (and other areas) the kind of effective independence they already had. And his accession was only with the approval of the people of his City (*LotR* 1991:III, 296-97). In other words, it is a case of local self-government (or subsidiarity) – most decisions are taken at the lowest possible level, closest to those who are most affected by them.[31]

This is the nature of the Shire as a yeoman-republic, including real connections to the tradition of civic republicanism, with its emphasis on a self-governing citizenry and its fear of corruption by clique and commerce. As Donald Davie (1973:93-94) noticed, the implication of *The Lord of the Rings* points firmly "towards the conviction that authority in public matters [...] can be and ought to be resisted and refused by anyone who wants to live humanely." This tradition has pre-modern roots, in Aristotle, Cicero and Machiavelli, but its contemporary relevance is none the less for that; and in no respect more importantly than to remind us that modern parliamentary liberalism has no franchise on democracy and community, or on solutions to our problems.[32]

Other societies in Middle-earth function differently still, although mostly under the aegis of non-autocratic royalty. Each is distinct, even among humans: Gondorians, the Riddermark and the Bree-folk are not interchangeable. Tolkien would have agreed with that humane and sceptical humanist – in an earlier and more honourable sense than the cult of 'reason', technology and Progress that it has now become – Hubert Butler (1986:95): "It is as neighbours, full of ineradicable prejudices, that we must love each other, and not as fortuitously 'separated brethren'." And indeed, *The Lord of the Rings* does hold out hope that very different kinds of traditions and

---

31 See Finch (1994:12-13), and Williams (1995:17, 19).
32 See Curry (1995), for an introduction.

communities can respect one another's differences and live at peace, without being subsumed into a vacuous Benneton-style multiculturalism dominated by American-led market forces: what Tom Shippey (1996) has aptly called 'burbocentrism'.

But none of these societies resemble Mordor: an utterly authoritarian state, with a slave-based economy centred on intensive industrialism and industrialised agriculture – "great slave-worked fields away south", while "in the northward regions were the mines and forges" (*LotR* 1991: III, 240) – all of which is directed towards the goal of global military domination. It is worth noting, too, given the cults of Hitler, Stalin and Mao (all leaders of supposedly secular states) that Mordor is also an "evil theocracy (for Sauron is also the god of his slaves) [...]" (*Letters* 1981:154). Once again, Tolkien has dared to offend modernist/humanist orthodoxy – or should I say, fantasy? – and name the truth.

To conflate Sauron with the pre-industrial kingships of Gondor or Rohan would thus be absurd. As Madawc Williams (1995:17) points out, "if one king feels morally bound to respect your existing rights while the other is planning either to enslave you or feed you to his Orcs, you'd have little trouble knowing which side you ought to be on!" Furthermore, what is «The Scouring of the Shire», politically speaking, but an account of local resistance to fascist thuggery and modernization?[33]

That leaves the "approval of traditional property settlements". Well, I doubt if Tolkien's approval could have been taken for granted; it would probably have depended a great deal on what was proposed for the land in question. And as Jonathan Bate (1991:46) points out, redistributing ownership is not going to be much use if the land in question is poisoned beyond use.

As I mentioned earlier, Bate (1991:11) makes another important point too: a distinction between love of the land and love of the fatherland. The former, which is clear both in Tolkien's personal life and his books, involves a fierce attachment to highly specific and local places and things.

---

33 See Plank (1975); he also points out that "Tolkien opposes fascism as a conservative rather than as a democrat" (1975:114).

As such, it offers little foothold to the inflated emotional abstractions that are so essential to nationalistic fascism. This is vividly illustrated in Sam's saving realization, when tempted by the Ring of Power, that "The one small garden of a free gardener was all his need and due, not a garden swollen to a realm; his own hands to use, not the hands of others to command" (*LotR* 1991: III, 210-11).

The Cultural Student

Williams was the chief founding father in this country (along with Hoggart) of what is now called cultural studies. One of its luminaries, and Williams's biographer in a work he himself describes as an act of homage, is Fred Inglis (1995, and see 1994). He wrote essays on Tolkien in 1981 and 1983. I will try to be brief, because I already addressed some of their content, but also because his work here plumbs such a nadir of mendacity.[34]

Inglis (1981:192) writes that Tolkien's prose "*is* moving, there is no doubt, but it moves a reader away from and never towards real life." "Real life" is a purely rhetorical gesture here, of course, signifying 'what us left-Leavisite Grown-Ups have, in our wisdom, decided is real'. But there is worse to come, for "Tolkien's 'schmaltz-Götterdammerung'" is such that "for once it makes sense to use that much-abused adjective, and call Tolkien a Fascist" (Inglis 1981:197). Williams, of course, implied the same; as have others: Jonathan Miller, for example, in a characteristically glib equation of Tolkien and Wagner.[35] Now, I have already shown the utter flimsiness of such a charge. In addition, there is simply no Wagnerian 'Götterdämmerung' in *The Lord of the Rings*; "Victory neither restores an earthly Paradise nor ushers in New Jerusalem" (Muirhead 1986:20). In addition, Tolkien

---

34 Although, to be fair, it is no worse than his editor and some of his fellow contributors to Giddings's (1983) execrable collection, thankfully already discussed by Colebatch (1990:67-81). See, e.g., the slimy sub-cultural materialism of Nigel Walmsley, Nick Otty's confusions about deconstruction and Brenda Partridge's dysfunctional psychoanalysis.

35 This is typical of Miller in its arrogance and ignorance, as so often when he ventures out of his area of actual expertise; but personal psychology apart, it also typifies the consequences of a dogmatic belief in the tenets of scientific secularism, rationalism and modernism.

strongly disliked Wagner, all the more so for drawing directly on some of the same mythological material that the latter only knew second-hand, and to such very different ends (see Shippey 1992:296). (Interestingly, Ragnarok was a relatively late aspect of Germano-Scandinavian mythology that never caught on in the pagan Anglo-Saxon England that so influenced Tolkien. Even then, it was, apparently, unEnglish in its melodrama [Branston 1957:155].)

Inglis makes a number of other bizarre assertions to back up his specious claim: "Like all popular cultures, Middle-earth's utopia is prehistoric and classless", his prose "abjures any corporeal solidity", being "bodiless", "colourless", and "unreally picturesque", and "none of his characters reflect on their actions for a moment". Overall, "the whole book is suffused with an intense spirituality which [...] transposes what is physical into the soaring splendours of musical experience which, having no referent, cannot *signify* but only move" (Inglis 1983:33, 35-37). I say "bizarre" because (1) again, there is no such utopia, at least in the sense Inglis means, and what is there is saturated with historicity; (2) it is precisely the corporeal reality of Middle-earth that impresses the overwhelming majority of readers; and (3) there is hardly a major character in the book who doesn't, at some point, reflect on his or her actions. (Inglis's utilitarian contempt for music speaks for itself.)

He comments that "Such a feeling does not transcend culture, it is created by culture" (Inglis 1983:33). Here we at least touch usefully on a fundamental flaw in cultural studies, which is to conclude that because something is learned, cultural, contingent or constructed it isn't real or true. Of course, by simply reversing the conservative valuation of instinctive, natural, necessary and revealed, the same impoverished oppositions are preserved intact, and any critical advance on them disabled. As Antony Easthope (1991:45) puts it, the "literature-as-construction analysis relies on an erroneous either/or: either literary value is a textual essence independent of the reader; or there is no literary value at all." Above all, to quote Derrida (1988:136), "All that ['quite simply everything'] is political, but it is not only political." Quite so. Tolkien's work cannot "transcend culture" in the way Inglis absurdly implies, because *no* discourse can. On the other hand, although "created by culture" it addresses a great deal more than that: nature, ethics, myth ...

But Inglis's chief strategy is carefully to condemn and disown a series of critical tactics before proceeding himself to turn them on Tolkien. Thus, he mocks the "old, round way of dealing with bestsellers", which viewed their readers as seeking refuge "in a fantasy world (swear word) whose emotional gratifications (ditto) compensated for (school-teacher's report judgement) the emptiness of everyday life (guerilla slogan)." Yet only a few pages later, we find a cringingly florid caricature of a 'typical' Tolkien reader – a former head of art in a market-town grammar-school, sitting in a new, pine-panelled unit in a converted farm building, reading Tolkien to his two young sons – doing exactly that (Inglis 1983:25, 27, 31-32).[36]

Inglis continues (1983:28) that "[t]o write of Tolkien's version of this tradition is not in the least to say that [...] [in] a now familiar but entirely empty putting-down, it is nostalgic [...]. *But*" – nonetheless – Tolkien's nostalgia "implies not only some distortion of vision but also a privileging of the past over the present such that the present can *only* be lived in terms of its failure to measure up to the past [...]." And his final disingenuous gesture is to retract his claim that Tolkien is a fascist, before asserting that his work is: "instead of Nuremberg, Frodo's farewell" – equally a travesty of the text and the history that as Clay Ramsay remarked, "Inglis uses on Tolkien apparently to situate him, but really to engulf him."[37]

The Psychoanalyst

It is almost a relief to turn to another of Tolkien's sternest critics, Rosemary Jackson, a literary critic with strong commitments to both Marxism and psychoanalysis. She believes that Middle-earth is somehow "outside the

---

36 As he (1983:3) himself admits, "Once we have set the irony-stereotypwriter to work, it is easy for any bookish person who lives within the London-Bristol ellipse of thriving capital to go on remorselessly in this vein." So why does he do so, and allow it to stand as substantive and fair comment?

37 Personal communication. (Typically, Inglis's determination to make his point overrides his 'grateful' acceptance of Claude Rawson's correction on this point in the *Times Literary Supplement* of 26.6.82 – (Inglis 1983:41, n. 18).

human [...] free from the demands of historical time, or of mortality" – which is presumably why "fairy tales discourage in the importance or effectiveness of action", and why those of Tolkien (together with C.S. Lewis and a host of other offenders) function "as conservative vehicles for social and instinctual repression [...] supporting a ruling ideology" and serving only to "reinforce a blind faith in 'eternal' moral values, really those of an outworn liberal humanism." In addition to the by-now-familiar charge of 'nostalgic', she attacks "the chauvinistic, totalitarian effects of [Tolkien's] vision [...]" and sympathizes with those victims of repression, the orcs, of whose hairiness (as a sign of desire) she makes much (1988:154-56).

Since Jackson too is fond of what she calls "reality", let us run a textual reality-check on her own claims. Tolkien's work is saturated with historicity – a claim which I submit to the judgement of any informed reader; "Death and the desire for deathlessness" was perhaps his most fundamental theme (see *Letters* 1981:262, 18); *The Lord of the Rings* is nothing if not packed with action, upon the outcomes of which everything subsequent hangs; and whatever the values inherent in his work – and liberal humanism is an odd description of them: Tolkien as E.M. Forster? – "outworn" would seem rather presumptuous in the light of their popular reception. As for the hairiness of Jacksons's orcs, what of hobbits' famously hairy feet? Or is that bourgeois hair?

Already by 1953, Kenneth Burke (1957:119) could justifiably complain that "people have gone on too long with the glib psychonalytic assumption that an art of 'escape' promotes acquiescence. It may, as easily, assist a reader to clarify his dislike of an environment in which he is placed." Three-and-a-half decades later, Jackson and most of Tolkien's other leading critics are still making the same glib assumption. And driving her Freudian anathema we find the same atavistic Enlightenment essentialism, with its faith in the power of Reason to liberate us from 'repressive energies' and attain utopia: "De-mystifying the process of reading fantasies will, hopefully, point to the possibility of *undoing* many texts which work, unconsciously, upon us." Why? Because "In the *end* this may lead to *real* social transformation" (Jackson 1988:10, my emphases).

Let us pause here, note the modernist profession of faith in demystification, and ask: what is this state of freedom, equally 'hors le texte' and the bonds of 'savoir/pouvoir', into which such "undoing" (magically uninfluenced by any new reading) releases us? Exactly what and when is this distinctly eschatological "end"? And what is this equally absolutist "real" transformation, as opposed to the kind we know from mere history and quotidian experience? In short, who is really the utopian fantasist here: Tolkien, or Jackson?

What *shouldn't* be utopian is to find not a nonpolitical criticism, certainly, but in Joan Acacella's words (1995:71) "a sophisticated criticism – one that, while indebted to a certain politics, can balance that concern with a sustained attention to what the artist is saying." But by now it should come as no surprise to find (as Attebery (1993:23) has pointed out) that Jackson also cites an essay by the politically acceptable W.H. Auden as the source of some of Tolkien's ideas in his «On Fairy-Stories», when the former appeared twenty-one years after the latter. (Valentine Cunningham (1989:232) recently performed a similar trick when using Auden's satire on "ruralizing simple-lifers" to sneer at Tolkien's "mythic and escapist fairyland". He conveniently fails to mention Auden's fulsome praise for *The Lord of the Rings*.)

Escapist?

This was a charge which recurs throughout the attacks of Tolkien's critics, and he was familiar with it early in his career. His essay «On Fairy-Stories» provides his own best defence. As an instance, Tolkien mentions the recent technological innovation (in his time) of mass-produced electric streetlamps. Any writer who ignores such developments, or prefers to discuss, say, lightning, is liable to be labelled escapist:

> out comes the big stick: 'Electric lamps have come to stay,' they say. [... Or:] 'The march of Science, its tempo quickened by the needs of war, goes inexorably on ... making some things obsolete, and foreshadowing new developments in the utilization of electricity': an advertisement. This says the same thing only more menacingly.
>
> («On Fairy-Stories», 1988:56)

The prison, to encapsulate my theme, is enforced modernity, whose human casualties alone now number in many millions, while for animals and the natural world the holocaust is still continuing. And its intellectual and cultural warders are the 'realists' and 'rationalists' whom Tolkien has in mind when he says, for example, that "The notion that motor-cars are more 'alive' than, say, centaurs or dragons is curious; that they are more 'real' than horses is pathetically absurd" («On Fairy-Stories», 1988:57). In the years before Nazism, Stalinism and Maoism provided such grim confirmation, and before global consumer capitalism took over the job, Tolkien already saw this clearly. Yet his only honour among the elites is still to be accounted escapist, juvenile and irrational. This, with Tolkien, I utterly deny:

> it is after all possible for a rational man, after reflection (quite unconnected with fairy-stories or romance), to arrive at the condemnation, implicit at least in the mere silence of 'escapist' literature, of progressive things like factories, or the machine-guns and bombs that appear to be their most natural and inevitable, dare we say 'inexorable', products.
>
> («On Fairy-Stories», 1988:58)

The Lord of the Rings is hardly escapist within its own context, either, centred as it is around a war, struggle, hardship and suffering. And at the end of his tale, occasional hints about other worlds notwithstanding, Tolkien returns us firmly to *this* one: at the Grey Havens, after the departure of Frodo and Gandalf, Sam "stood far into the night, hearing only the sigh and murmur of the waves on the shores of Middle-earth, and the sound of them sank deep into his heart" (*LotR* 1991:III, 378). We stand with him. At best, Tolkien's 'evangelium' permits only a "fleeting glimpse of Joy" in this world, not permanent transportation to the next («On Fairy-Stories», 1988:62). The nostalgia he engenders, therefore, is finally redirected back into our own lives here. In Geoffrey Grigson's still more compact words:

> be comforted.
> Content I did not say.

The Structuralist

Christine Brooke-Rose is an eminent structuralist, professor of literature in Paris, and author of experimental modernist novels.[38] Here again, we find the heavy guns of Theory employed not to comprehend Tolkien but to get rid of him. Gimli and Legolas serve "no functional role [...] [and are] wholly gratuitous". Any maps and appendices are mere "semiological compensation". And *The Lord of the Rings*'s histories and genealogies are "not in the least necessary to the narrative, but they have given much infantile happiness to the Tolkien clubs and societies [...]" (Brooke-Rose 1981:237-38, 247).

The modernist dread of being thought infantile shared by Wilson and Brooke-Rose seems to be related to a widespread contempt for Tolkien's "fans" (almost always "fans", perhaps to invoke an implicit association with something like football). The editor of one book of scholarly (but mostly dull) essays on Tolkien (Isaacs and Zimbardo 1981:2) poisonously dismisses as "fanfluff" publications by Tolkien societies that contain very little worse and not a little that is better.[39] Tolkien himself, as Carpenter (1992:233) writes, once "referred to the widespread enthusiasm for his books as 'my deplorable cultus'". Yet the objects of this fastidiousness are readers for whom Tolkien's work is large and alive, and who are therefore better-placed to understand it than his narrowly scholarly dissectors. It is the latter who deserve pity and scorn.

Like Jackson, Brooke-Rose puts *The Lord of the Rings* through the structuralist text-grinder in order (she supposes) to attain freedom through disenchantment. Another practitioner, Nick Otty (1983:155), similarly recommends 'deconstructing' *The Lord of the Rings* "so that we may see the

---

38 The latter, persistently unpopular, were recently defended by Lorna Sage in the *Times Literary Supplement* (12.8.94), who wrote that Brooke-Rose's "voice has seemed more distant and characterless than in fact it is" – something to treasure alongside Mark Twain's observation, more deliberately ironic, that Wagner's music "is better than it sounds."

39 Such as the (UK) Tolkien Society's *Mallorn* and the (USA) Mythopoeic Society's *Mythlore*, *Arda* (Sweden) and *Lembas* (Netherlands). This is evidently an attitude shared even by Rosebury (1992:129); but not, I'm glad to say, by Shippey or Attebery.

text as a construct produced in a certain context", and are therefore "no longer 'in thrall' to it" – an ambition whose risibility I have already discussed.[40] All that distinguishes Brooke-Rose's (1980) version is its detailed and dismal emphasis on "the machinery of realism", "mechanisms inherent to the marvellous", and so on. I am forcibly reminded of Treebeard's description of Saruman: "He has a mind of metal and wheels, and he does not care for growing things [...]" (*LotR* 1991:II, 90). This is no mere conceit: structuralism, like Marxism and psychoanalysis, bears a heavy freight of what Howard Felperin (1985:57) called "a lingering nineteenth-century faith or superstition – that the study of literary texts can be, should be, or, in the case of their own work, *is* scientific."[41]

No wonder, then, that Brooke-Rose (1981:237-38, 244-45, 247) cannot seem to comprehend Tolkien, or indeed, even *read* him: "orks" – "the Gollum" – "Tolkien's trilogy" – "Sam Gamjee" – "Elf-people" – "Belin" (for Balin) – "Edora" – "Minas Mogul" – "Moria Mountain". (Edmund Wilson had already saved her some time with "Gandalph" and "dwarfs", and Stimpson with "Sarumen".) She gives the wizards their own language, states that Gandalf, "although a wizard, can only perform minor magic" (!), and has Arwen's father Elrond as her brother.[42] The sloppiness of such an astounding catalogue of errors, and the arrogance it implies, would hardly be tolerated in other areas of scholarly inquiry, and it speaks volumes about Brooke-Rose's (and her publisher's) attitude to her subject.

A Literary-Industrial Establishment

Brooke-Rose's attitude is also part of a larger critical problem in relation to the whole genre that Tolkien's success unintentionally created. Consider,

---

40 See my remarks on Jackson, above. (It is equally amusing to find him complaining about Tolkien's "fusion and confusion of levels of reality" and narratives – unlike, say, that of Borges, O'Brien or Calvino?)

41 Note too the cultural studies mantra of 'interrogating' texts, which reveals a common mentality if not indeed origin in the Baconian interrogation of nature, bound and on the rack.

42 Some of Brooke-Rose's mistakes are mentioned in Rosebury (1992:154); and see Shippey (1992:282-84).

for example, how mainstream literati lapped up the magic and spirituality of South and Central American and African 'magic realism' because it seemed exotic, while condemning to the 'fantasy' ghetto any local and native expressions of the same. Alternatively an author identified as a mainstream novelist is frequently praised for imaginative daring when he or she incorporates fantasy into a novel, but authors who have been pigeon-holed as fantasy-writers can do the same thing (only better) in vain.[43] And any fantasy-writer with a local product that threatens to succeed more widely is firmly slapped down with the usual modernist cliches: "childish", "phantastic", and partaking of an "underlying irrationality" which is "okay" in poetry and children's writing, but not "in a grown-up novel for grown-ups" (Turner 1996). This is not reviewing, it is policing.

Such an attitude was early and aptly analyzed by Walter Benjamin, in a wonderful essay entitled «The Storyteller», whose every resonance applies to Tolkien. He noted that

> the art of storytelling is coming to an end. Less and less frequently do we encounter people with an ability to tell a tale properly. More and more often there is embarrassment all around when the wish to hear a story is expressed. [...] The art of storytelling is reaching its end because the epic side of truth, wisdom, is dying out. [...] A great storyteller will always be rooted in the people, primarily in a milieu of craftsmen. [...] The fairy tale, which to this day is the first tutor of children because it was the first tutor of mankind, secretly lives on in the story.
>
> (Benjamin 1969:83, 87, 101, 102)[44]

---

43 E.g. high praise for Mark Helprin's "literary" *Winter's Tale* (1983) but ignoring John Crowley's superior 'fantasy' *Little, Big* (1982), for Deepak Chopra's New Age *The Return of Merlin* (1995) but not Robert Holdstock's genuinely chthonic *Mythago Wood* (1982), and so on.

44 Benjamin's modernist admirers, at least those who have also engaged in Tolkien criticism, seem to have missed this essay. I am very grateful to Nicola Bown for bringing it to my attention.

Benjamin described the novel as a huge step away from storytelling, with its roots in the oral tradition; the modern obsession with information is yet another huge removal. And the novels are bad enough: permitted only

> that necessary degree of irony which is the sole form of 'honesty' modern prose styles or conventions readily allow. [...] Unhappy with myth, wary of emotion, harried by empty political terminologies, scornful of 'character', eager, it seems, to refine, redefine and narrow down the material until the works in question are about themselves, nothing else but themselves. Affirmation, no. Consolation, certainly not.

(Potter 1984:12-13, 31)[45]

No wonder that, as Tolkien (*Letters* 1981:209) believed, "the 'fairy-story' is really an adult genre, and one for which a starving audience exists."

This *trahison* of readers by the clerks is one in which critics colloborate with writers and publishers. If, as Brian Attebery (1992:17) suggests, "the task of literary theory is to provide a framework capable of accounting for the story's success in its own terms, rather than denying that its aims are achievable or worth the attempt", then literary theory has dismally failed with Tolkien, and fantasy literature in general. Indeed, as Bill Buford (1996:11-12) recently pointed out, in the 1,383 pages of the authoritative *New Princeton Encyclopedia of Poetry and Poetics*, there is no entry for 'story'! In the book pages of the quality press, the situation is no better. Those calling the shots include people like Martin Amis, self-consciously clever modernist 'par excellence', for *The Sunday Times*; and Robert McCrum, for *The Observer*, who seems to view Marx and America with equal reverence (and no sense of contradiction).[46]

---

45 The depressing degeneration of Italo Calvino's fiction is a characteristic case in point.

46 Amis's attitude to anything at odds with the modernist credo was perhaps revealed by his 'review' for the *London Review of Books* of Robert Bly's *Iron John* – a book which, whatever else one might think of it, at least raised serious and interesting issues. The entire piece consisted of variations on sniggering occasioned by Bly's title denoting a gay man in Amis's boyhood English slang.
Asked in a recent interview in the *New Statesman and Society* (3.5.1996), "Which books and authors have had the greatest influence on your political beliefs?" McCrum replied "*The Communist Manifesto* and *The Eighteenth Brumaire* by Karl Marx." Yet "Which event during your lifetime has had the greatest effect on your political beliefs?" "My first

Now that Seamus Heaney has won the Nobel prize for Literature, will it begin to dawn that as he remarked, "the movement is always from delight to wisdom and not vice versa"? I doubt it. As much as ever it remains the case, to quote Nuala O'Faolain, writing in *The Irish Times* (7.11.1992), that

> [t]he language of highbrow criticism can only cope with a certain kind of fiction. It has no vocabulary with which to discuss a world where neither the individual nor the society is self-conscious, and the author pretends not to be either. [...] The ordinary reader is far ahead of the critics in ease with such a world.

This in turn relates to the 'déformation professionelle' of modern criticism, journalism and publishing as a whole – aggressively secular, cynical, snobbish and incestuous – which is beyond my scope here.[47] But I will give Karel Capek, writing in *PEN International* (45.1, 1995), the last word on the subject:

> look how often the cultural world pronounces a sentence of annihilating rejection. How old-fashioned ideas, other people's views, or those of the habitues of a different literary cafe, are arrogantly dismissed out of hand. [...] This is variously called literary criticism, ideological struggle, a matter of principle, or the generation gap. In truth it is merely prickly intellectual exclusiveness running around looking for something to turn its nose up at. If your nose is in the air, though, you cannot see properly.

Nor can you read very well.

Why?

The question remains: how could so many otherwise intelligent critics be so slapdash, unfair and just plain wrong? First, let's notice that they are so in

---

visit to America in 1976 showed me how it was possible to live in a genuinely free society."

47 On a "snide and aggressive" media, see Gopnik (1994:84-102); also Nicholson-Lord (1995), and Midgeley (1997).

significantly similar ways. The specific charges against Tolkien and the values in whose name they are made make up a strong family resemblance, and I have suggested we call it modernism. Indeed, Williams's Marx, Jackson's Freud, Brooke-Rose's Saussure – these are among the very avatars of modernism, whose 'grand narratives' of modernity – secularised versions of divine revelation – were supposed to supply essentially complete accounts of our progress towards the realisation of the truth. But there have been too many broken promises by now, and too many terrible 'successes'. The human being has become a stranger not only to the cosmos and the Earth but to each other, and him- and herself. By now, "man himself has become, after God and nature, an anthropomorphism" (Schnadelbach 1992:314).

Modernism is not the only description possible; another strong candidate I have already mentioned is humanism, as analyzed in David Ehrenfeld's *The Arrogance of Humanism* (1978) – a book which, not coincidentally, cites or quotes Tolkien approvingly several times. On balance, however, I think the former term has the edge. But in either case, Tolkien's apostasy (or perhaps more properly, since he never subscribed to it in the first place, heresy) often seems so strongly felt by true believers as actively to interfere with being able actually to read him. As J.P. Stern once remarked, "Contempt is a poor guide." The modernist missionaries arrive in Middle-earth dressed in a space-suit of Theory, protected from contamination by what they have already decided is its infantilism, escapism and reactionary politics. This is hardly good critical practice; can you imagine any of them admitting with William Empson, writing in the *London Review of Books* (4.2.1988), that "A literary critic must be prepared to say, 'This is good, though I don't know why; not yet anyhow' [...]"? Or finding it in their hearts to say a good word – on any grounds whatever – about Wodehouse, Kipling or Yeats? Yet Orwell somehow managed it, without losing his socialist soul.[48]

---

48 See, by contrast, Raymond Williams's biographical attack on Orwell – a perfect sample of dogmatic socialist sanctimony.

But the modernists are right, in their own twisted way. *The Lord of the Rings* really is a text whose predominant available meanings powerfully contradict their own values;[49] and whose popular success, as a sign of widely shared doubts if not repudiation, makes it, from their point of view, all the worse. In the intention of its author an *anti*-modernist text, attacking industrialism, secularism, and the myth of Progress, *The Lord of the Rings* falls into the traditions of what Jonathan Bate (1991) calls "romantic ecology", Don Elgin (1985) "the ecological perspective of comedy" and Meredith Veldman (1994) "Romantic Protest". And like the works of other such authors – William Wordsworth, John Ruskin, William Morris – it has acquired powerful new meanings in a *post*-modern context.[50] When this dimension overlaps with Tolkien's enduring popularity in the same way as that of Dickens, Kipling and Hardy, you get some idea of the potential power of his books – and of the critics' irresponsibility in so cavalierly dismissing them.

Of course, as both Shippey and Rosebury have pointed out, there are important modern elements in Tolkien's work: its stress on the anti-heroic and unmilitary hobbits and their reluctant participation (and that of others, such as Faramir and indeed Aragorn; the martial Boromir comes to a bad end) in the War of the Ring; war itself as at best a necessary evil; its Actonian view of power (in the Ring) as unavoidably corrupting; and even its absence of explicit religion.[51] But Tolkien's very syncretism offends modernist purism.

Ironically, therefore, it is his critics who belong to the past, and Tolkien the future. It is they who are nostalgic for the past, including their role as legislators (in Zygmunt Bauman's terms) rather than the interpreters they have become. Behind their instinctive antagonism lies an

---

49 As was noticed by Wilson (1974:37), *The Lord of the Rings* "is at once an attack on the modern world and a credo, a manifesto."

50 Veldman's book (1994) shows connections between Tolkien's popularity and the CND/END protest movement that far outweigh E.P.Thompson's superficial use of imagery from his books to describe a Cold War mentality – something about which he was corrected (as he later acknowledged) by Jessica Yates; see her article «Tolkien the Anti-totalitarian» (Yates 1995).

51 See Rosebury (1992:148) and Shippey (1992:24).

uncomfortable sense that here is a coherent fictional critique and alternative, in every major respect, to the exhausted myth of modernity which has so far underwritten their own professional status; and worse still, it is a popular one. Not for the first time, those who claim to speak for universal truth and reason are lagging behind 'the people' whom they often claim to represent, and whose interests to know better than the people themselves.[52]

Now, it is perfectly possible to imagine Tolkien's books 'being' truly reactionary: racist, nationalist, etc. – that is, having those kinds of effects. In fact, there is one historical instance of just that, when his writings were briefly adopted by some violent right-wingers in Italy who held a 'Camp Hobbit' outside Rome in June 1978.[53] What I am arguing, however, is that (1) neither in his intention nor (especially) essentially or inherently is Tolkien's work pathologically reactionary; and that (2) *as it happens* – as things have actually turned out – his implicit diagnosis of modernity was prescient; and his vision of an alternative, progressive. (Of course, it also follows that his critics, despite their loud claims to being both, were neither.)

Thus, in the context of global modernisation and the resistance to it, his stories have become an animating and inspiring new myth. It is one that suggests that just as there was life before modernity, so there can be after it. They are deeply nostalgic, certainly; but it is an emotionally empowering nostalgia, not a crippling one. And it joins up with a growing contemporary sense, represented in postmodernism, of history's sheer contingency – the liberating perception that it-might-have-been-different, and therefore *could* be different now.[54]

---

52 Another good example: the attempt by modernists like Waldemar Januszczak and Martin Pawley to trash the doubts, fears and dislike of much modern architecture by Prince Charles in 1989-90. They invoked everything from the size of his ears, and associations with Hitler to economic 'realism' and 'progress'. But the vast outpouring in the media from members of the public in Charles' defence demonstrated that he was, overwhelmingly, speaking for them; and to those feelings, the experts had no convincing reply.

53 See Bjorgo (1995:234), who cites Franco Ferreresi (ed.), *La Destra Radicale*. I am grateful to Matthew Kalman for this reference.

54 For a brilliant essay on Middle-earth as a 'Fourth World' Europe, unstained by industrialism and imperialism, see Luling (1995).

Post/Modernity and Re-Enchantment

By modernism I mean not so much a particular literary or artistic or architectural movement as the self-conscious articulation and celebration of the chief values and goals of modernity. And by modernity I mean the co-dependent power of corporate and finance capital, the modern political state and modern science that is probably best summed up in Lewis Mumford's term, "the megamachine". These have generated, and are served by, the ideologies of economism, statism and scientism. The last, particularly relevant to us here, is the belief that only science, being dis- or un-enchanted, has access to the truth; it is therefore the only legitimate kind of knowledge, to the exclusion (and if possible elimination) of all others, e.g. traditional and local forms (see Ekins 1992). A primary commitment is thus to deny and/or disguise the fact that science, as an epistemological practice, is no less a contingent and fallible human construct than any other kind; in other words, that even science is not 'scientific' in the way they mean it.[55]

Modernity began to grow in the late seventeenth century, received clear and programmatic articulation in the Enlightenment of the eighteenth century, developed powerful new political and economic forms in the nineteenth, and attained truly global dimensions of natural and social engineering in the twentieth (see Toulmin 1990). Its chief characteristics – historically formed, but nonetheless essential for that – can be defined as *monism* and *universalism*: truth, initially divine and apprehended through revelation, but then (without significant modification of its 'modus operandi') secular and apprehended through reason, that is single and universal. And this truth must be certain; hence the modernist obsession with 'theoria', or science, going back to Descartes, Galileo, Bacon and Hobbes. (Toulmin identifies these men as instituting a "counter-enlightenment" to the earlier pre-modern humane scepticism of Montaigne and Erasmus.)

---

55 In addition to Paul Feyerabend's books, see recent work in the history and sociology of science – e.g. by Stephen Shapin and Simon Schaffer, to mention only two names out of many – as well as the new growth industry of attempting to debunk this work by scientific publicists.

As Kolakowski points out, the origins of this modernity can be dated back as far as the eleventh century; but

> the question so many of us have been trying to cope with is not so much when modernity started, but what is the core – whether or not explicitly expressed – of our contemporary widespread 'Unbehagen in der Kultur'? [...] And the first answer that naturally comes to mind is summed up, of course, in the Weberian 'Entzauberung' – disenchantment – or in any similar word roughly covering the same phenomenon.
> (Kolakowski 1990:7)

The characteristic rhetorical gesture of modernism – its sacrament, one might say – is indeed unmasking, demystifying, debunking, and indeed destroying false gods, false truths, false consciousness. The trouble is, this process recognizes no limits; hence the power granted to its economic expression, neo-liberal market-forces, to tear up and make over everything – nature, communities, human nature. Without limits, however – which must therefore come from other sources – the terminus of this process is natural impoverishment, social violence and cultural nihilism (see Gray 1995).

Since my focus here is primariy cultural, let me illustrate the last by quoting art critic Sarah Kent, a big fan of the feted corpse-artist Damien Hirst. Extolling an exhibition of life-size castrated and mutilated dummies, she wrote: "They satisfy your [sic] blood-lust, they seduce, and they make you sick. Brilliant."[56] This sort of thing is sometimes backed-up with aesthetic theory, e.g. Bernstein (1996:16):

> Art cannot avoid the progressive disenchantment of the world that has occurred outside art; if it sought to obtain authenticity and authority for itself by summoning dead gods and dead meanings into its precincts, it would rightly be accused of naivete or anachronism. [...] Authenticity without cruelty is no longer possible.

And indeed, just these accusations are frequently levelled against *The Lord of the Rings* (including an unconscionable lack of cruelty).

---

56 From *Time Out* (5-12.10.1994).

But who says the gods and meanings to which it refers are dead, and on what warrant? Whether historically or metaphysically, it takes a peculiarly narrow and teleological modernism to assign them to the grave, only to be perpetually amazed at "the return of the repressed". In Russell Hoban's (1992:138) words, "Why cannot any god die? Because gods do not replace one another [...] gods are a cumulative projection of everything in us."[57] And as Tolkien long ago noted,

> the true road of escape from such weariness is not to be found in the wilfully awkward, clumsy, or misshapen, not in making all things dark or unremittingly violent; nor in the mixing of colours on through subtlety to drabness, and the fantastical complication of shapes to the point of silliness and on towards delirium. Before we reach such states we need recovery. We should look at green again, and be startled anew (but not blinded) by blue and yellow and red.
> («On Fairy-Stories», 1988:53)

And that is why, rather than a still further disenchantment that ends by eating itself, and utterly capitulating to the logic of capital and the market (art and otherwise), re-enchantment is needed: as Ted Hughes (1992) recently argued, the whole point of art is "to reopen negotiations with the mythic plane". The implication, which I shall not try to follow up here, is that postmodernists' militant secularism (such as that of Richard Rorty) actually disables their own programme.

Nonetheless, the basic critique of modernity (including its articulations in modernism) which has come to be called postmodernism is correct as far as it goes. It has been aptly summed up by Barbara Hernnstein Smith (1988:179) as "intellectual/ political totalitarianism (the effort to identify the presumptively universally compelling Truth and Way and to compel it universally) [...]".[58] The essence of this programme is not

---

[57] He adds, "I'm not trying to reduce this to psychiatry – I mean that we worship the gods projected by the god-force that projects us as well on the screen of its mind."

[58] Cf. Laclau and Mouffe (1985:191-92): "This point is decisive: there is no radical and plural democracy without renouncing the discourse of the universal, and its implicit assumption of a privileged point of access to 'the truth', which can only be reached by a limited number of subjects."

rationality 'per se', "but a deranged, totalizing rationalism which yields disenchantment", whose products include, as Max Weber foresaw (and some of whom I have already quoted), "[s]pecialists without spirit, sensualists without heart; this nullity imagines that it has attained a level of civilization never before achieved" (Kontos 1994:235, 233). Modernity therefore need not, indeed cannot be countered with mere irrationality. Culturally speaking, these exemplars of nullity may now simply and without any regrets be abandoned:

> The growing sense that we are not bound to *complete* the project of modernity (Habermas' phrase) and still do not necessarily have to lapse into irrationality or into apocalyptic frenzy, the sense that art is not exclusively pursuing some telos of abstraction, non-representation, and sublimity – all of this has opened up a host of possibilities for creative endeavors today.
> (Huyssen 1986:217)

Nor is postmodernity a new era marking the end of modernity or even modernism; but it does articulate a process in which hitherto largely unquestioned modernist truths look increasingly, to increasing numbers of people, like highly questionable assumptions. And people *do* have questions – more people, with more and deeper fears and worries, than perhaps ever before. By now, only a fool (or convert, or employee) would say they are groundless.

By contrast, then, the chief characteristics of postmodernism – as an articulation of postmodernity – are *pluralism, localism,* and *perspectivism* (or "relativism").[59] As against the quest for certainty, there is room for Keats's negative capability, that is, "capable of being in uncertainties, mysteries, doubts, without any irritable reaching after fact and reason." The postmodern question is not 'is it true?' but 'is it any use?'; its 'modus vivendi', accordingly, is not theory but the 'practical wisdom' of 'phronesis'. And its proper cultural project, in response to modernist nihilism (or what Michael Ende (1993) calls "the Nothing") is *re-*

---

59 These can be summed up as "anti-essentialism".

enchantment: what Tolkien («On Fairy-Stories», 1988:18) described as "the primal desire at the heart of Faerie: the realization, independent of the conceiving mind, of imagined wonder." But the "realization" here is ambiguous, and properly so; it signifies both the making of the natural world wonderous through the creation of a "Secondary World [...] artistic in desire and purpose" («On Fairy-Stories», 1988:49), *and* the realization (through the former) that the Primary or 'real' world actually is wondrous.[60] Ultimately it has to be that way, for to adopt wonder as a way to save the world merely re-admits humanist utilitarianism by the back door.

Such project cannot succeed as an act purely or even primarily of will, because that is precisely the domain not of enchantment but of magic, which (in Tolkien's words) "is not an art but a technique; its desire is *power* in this world, domination of things and wills" («On Fairy-Stories», 1988:49-50). Thus "Faerie itself may perhaps most nearly be translated by Magic – but it is magic of a peculiar mood and power, at the furthest pole from the vulgar devices of the laborious, scientific, magician" («On Fairy-Stories», 1988:15). Tolkien's intuition here is historically borne out by modern science's continuity with, and largely unacknowledged borrowings from, magic.[61] And why it cannot save us now is that together with capital and the state, such science is what has created this crisis.

Aspects of postmodernism that are most relevant here have been voiced by Paul Feyerabend (1987:89) – "we either call gods and quarks equally real, but tied to different sets of circumstances, or we altogether cease talking about the 'reality' of things and use more complex ordering schemes instead" – and Zygmunt Bauman (1992:x-xi):

> Above all, postmodernity can be seen as restoring to the world what modernity, presumptuously, had taken away; as a re-enchantment of the world that modernity had tried hard to disenchant. [...] The war against mystery and magic was for modernity the war of liberation leading to the declaration of reason's independence. [...] world had to be de-spiritualized,

---

60 The point about (re-)enchantment not being a matter of will was also asserted to me, in conversation, by Roberto Calasso.

61 Out of a vast literature, see Webster (1982).

de-animated: denied the capacity of subject. [...] It is against such a disenchanted world that the postmodern re-enchantment is aimed.

But note that we are not comparing a prior or later state of enchantment (what Tolkien identifies as "Faerie") with one of disenchantment; that concedes far too much to the disingenuous mythology of modernism, which pretends it is fundamentally different. Recalling Tolkien's distinction between magic and enchantment permits us to recognize what such scientists are doing, and their representives defending, for what it is, namely modernist magic: a powerful negative or *counter*-enchantment, much of whose power stems from being a spell that denies that it is one, a secular religion – literally a bad faith, born of Descartes's dream (again, literally) of a perfect and certain knowledge that has culminated in the avowal of Edward Teller, 'father' of the hydrogen bomb, that "There is no case where ignorance should be preferred to knowledge [...]". That may well be true for science; it is by no means always true for humanity. With better reason than he knows, Teller's interviewer described him as "our great master of the black art of detachment".[62]

That is why modernists cannot afford to take myth, folk-tale and fantasy seriously, and find any serious exemplars or discussion thereof offensive and even threatening. As Le Guin (1989:36) notes of fantasy, "It isn't factual, but it's true. Children know that. Adults know it too, and that is precisely why many of them are afraid of fantasy." To admit that would come perilously close to admitting the possibility that their own 'factual' truths partake of a perverted and disguised mythicity.

A note of clarification is appropriate, however. My critique of modernism and secularism should not be taken to imply advocacy of a return, somehow, to past religious certainties; and for these cogent reasons: (1) such a thing is impossible; (2) any such attempt is therefore bound to end up in the grossly distorted form of religious fundamentalism; and above all, (3) even if it were possible it would be highly undesirable. The fact is that modernist monism and universalism has its roots firmly in the

---

62 Hitchens (1994:45).

universalist monotheism of the Judaeo-Christian tradition, and its logic is essentially the same. The minimal requirements for an enchanted world, in which nature is respected as alive, integral and active, are "mystery and a plurality of spirits"; whereas a single god, as Max Weber realized, establishes a monopoly which implies that everything can be subjected to a single, 'rational', and therefore disenchanted ordering (Kontos 1994: 226ff).[63] 'Returning to God' therefore offers no solutions to the problems of modernity; quite the contrary. The only real advance is to a pluralist, locally-rooted, and 'relativist' re-enchantment that is *new*.

Nor do I equate enchantment with all that is good. But I do maintain that in some form or other, it is humanly unavoidable; and that critique which rejects scientific essentialism must address itself not to which discourses are truths and which merely narratives/stories/myths, but to which of the latter are helpful and which are not. I need hardly add, I hope, that if there is no master-template of single, universal and unenchanted Truth, then it follows that you are left with various and plural truths – *not*, as some would disingenuously have it, nothing but lies.

Richard Kearney is right (1985:78): "It is our ethical duty to use our powers of 'logos' to discriminate between the authentic and inauthentic uses to which 'mythos' is put in our culture." But the irony is that you cannot even begin to distinguish pathological myth from healthy and encourage the latter until you have admitted its reality and, when healthy, desirability. Dogmatic secularists and atheists stigmatize all forms alike and attempt to force an impossible (and undesirable) universal disenchantment; thus, failing to understand the legitimacy of the desire for (re-)enchantment as such, and wasting their fire on harmless or healthy kinds, they leave us more exposed than ever to its pathologies. Hence, in part, Tolkien's («On Fairy-Stories», 1988:45) insistence that "Fantasy is a rational not an irrational activity." But rational, appropriately, in the ancient (and postmodern) sense of 'phronesis', not 'theoria'. As Milton Scarborough (1994:110) writes,

---

63 This idea relates fundamentally to the "value pluralism" of Isaiah Berlin, itself deriving from Machiavelli.

The ultimate assessment of myth must be of a kind suited to the nature of myth as giving expression to apprehensions of the life-world and as functioning to provide an orientation for living in that world. Within those strictures myth is neither true nor false *in a theoretical sense* but viable or not viable for the tasks (both theoretical and otherwise) which confront us. This viability is not determined in intellectual terms but in the very process of living, by whether or not one is energized, whether or not problems are being solved, whether or not life is integrated at a variety of levels, whether or not it is endowed with a significance that pulls one toward the future in hope.

Back to Fantasy

All this has very specific and significant implications for fantasy literature in general and Tolkien's books in particular, which speak powerfully to precisely our present conditions. Drawing on the power of ancient Indo-European myth, they invite the reader into a compelling and remarkably complete pre-modern world, saturated with corresponding earlier values, which therefore feels something like a lost home. They are just the values whose jeopardy we most now feel: relationships of respect with each other, and nature, and (for want of a better word) the spirit, which have not been stripped of personal integrity and responsibility and decanted into a soulless calculus of financial profit-and-loss. Wisdom in Middle-earth is not a matter of economic, scientific or technological expertise, but of practical and ethical maturity. If Middle-earth had a prophet, he was John Ruskin (1862, quoted in Wilmer 1985:222): "THERE IS NO WEALTH BUT LIFE." And:

> To watch the corn grow, and the blossoms set; to draw hard breath over ploughshare or spade; to read, to think, to love, to hope, to pray, – these are the things that make men happy; they have always had the power of doing these, they never *will* have the power to do more. The world's prosperity or adversity depends upon our knowing and teaching these few things: but upon iron, or glass, or electricity, or steam, in no wise.

(Ruskin 1856, quoted in Bate 1991:81)

But this same world, as we begin *The Lord of the Rings*, is under severe threat from those who worship pure power, and are therefore its slaves – the technological and instrumental power embodied in Sauron (after whom the book itself is named, after all), and the epitome of modernism gone mad. Reading this story, one therefore finds oneself reading our own story. That is one reason why so many readers have taken it so to heart. Another is that just as Sauron is vanquished in *The Lord of the Rings* – albeit barely, temporarily, and at great cost – so Tolkien, crucially, offers his readers *hope* that what is precious and threatened in our world might survive too.

Only those who cling to the modernist myth of a singular universal truth – as opposed to myth and story and indeed interpretation as such, which is somehow directly accessible to those with the 'correct' understanding – only these will look at Tolkien's glorious tree and see (to use an apt image of William Blake's) only "a green thing standing in the way." To the modernist, the choice is between Truth and myth (or falsehood). Whereas the postmodernist, giving up the pretense of a direct line to the Truth, sees the choice as between truths; or to put it another way, between myths (or stories) that are creative and liberating, and those that are destructive and debilitating.

So, for example, what really matters about the image of pre-Conquest England "as a free and equal rural community" benefitting from "a primitive freedom [and] the perpetual impulse and teaching of 'Nature'" (in Williams's (1985:79) excellent description) is not the extent to which things were 'actually' otherwise – though that too, itself an interpretation rather than a 'fact', may become mobilised as a resource in one political direction or another – but the *use* of such an image in the present. In his own way, Tolkien («On Fairy-Stories», 1988:32) himself saw this clearly: "When we have done all that research [...] can do [...] there remains still a point too often forgotten: that is the effect produced *now* by these old things in the stories as they are." Indeed, Tolkien's anti-positivism is bizarrely in tune with some of the best and most refreshing aspects of postmodern philosophy:

> You call a tree a tree [...] and you think nothing more of the word. But it was not a 'tree' until someone gave it that name.

You call a star a star, and say it is just a ball of matter moving on a mathematical course. But that is merely how *you* see it. By so naming things and describing them you are only inventing your own terms about them. And just as speech is invention about objects and ideas, so myth is invention about truth.
(Carpenter 1992:151)

Furthermore, "[t]he incarnate mind, the tongue, and the tale are in our world coeval", and "History often resembles 'Myth', because they are both ultimately of the same stuff" («On Fairy-Stories», 1988:24, 31). As for the Derridean endless flux of discourse, fairy-stories "have a greater sense and grasp of the endlessness of the World of Story than most modern 'realistic' stories, already hemmed within the narrow confines of their own small time" («On Fairy-Stories», 1988:72).[64]

This resonance is less surprising if one recalls that Tolkien was strongly influenced by Owen Barfield's *Poetic Diction. A Study in Meaning* (1928).[65] In a more recent adumbration, Barfield (1977:41) concluded that "Literalness is a quality which some words have achieved in the course of their history; it is not a quality with which the first words were born. [...] [The word 'literal'] means something which is the end-product of a long historical process." Furthermore, "[a]bandoning the specter of born literalness, we shall also abandon the whole dream of fixed entities with which literal meanings must somehow correspond."

Compare this with Laclau and Mouffe (1985:111): "Literality is, in actual fact, the first of metaphors." Or Paul Veyne (1988:38): "the flowering of myth and all manner of foolish tales ceases to mystify us by its gratuitousness and uselessness if we see that history itself is ceaseless invention and does not lead the reasonable life of a petty economizer." And it would be possible to quote any number of other authors to the same

---

64 Most recently, in his *Spectres of Marx* (1994), Derrida has written of the "infinite promise" of emancipation, which always risks betrayal through a vulgar and literal-minded realization. But isn't this what Tolkien meant by the hope of Escape – from modernity, from poverty and injustice, and from death itself – which runs exactly the same risk: e.g., in the last instance, the attempt at "endless serial living"? If so, how delicious an anticipation!

65 See the fascinating recent discussion by Hipolito (1993).

effect, questioning the naive reality of 'the real' and demonstrating the inescapability of metaphoric interpretation. Furthermore, this is the point at which myth, as one particularly powerful kind thereof, starts to become an enormous and fascinating subject which should at this point be addressed; but cannot be, here. For now, let us just note with Tolkien that

> Fantasy is a natural human activity. It certainly does not destroy or even insult Reason. [...] On the contrary. The keener and clearer is the reason, the better fantasy it will make. If men were ever in a state in which they did not want to know or could not perceive truth (facts or evidence), then Fantasy would languish [...] and become Morbid Delusion.
> For creative Fantasy is founded upon the hard recognition that things are so in the world as it appears under the sun; on a recognition of fact, but not a slavery to it.
> («On Fairy-Stories», 1988:51)

He rightly adds that "If men really could not distinguish between frogs and men, fairy-tales about frog-kings would not have arisen." It is thus the vulgar 'scientific' and 'materialist' literalists who have an interest in destroying metaphor and the creativity – in science no less than art and play – upon which, as Tolkien correctly notes, it depends.[66]

For closely related reasons, postmodernism has also restored the crucial importance of narrative, the way by which we produce and find meaning.[67] Thus, Brian Attebery (1992:40-41) has suggested that "Postmodernism is a return to storytelling in the belief that we can be sure of nothing but story." He (1992:46) shrewdly adds not only that postmodernist criteria are much better suited to explaining Tolkien's success than are realist or modernist criteria, but that fantasy "makes its metafictional statements most effectively when it seems most ingenuous, as in Tolkien's perfectly sincere, perfectly impossible narrative." By contrast, the tedious authorial reminders of textual artificiality that are often

---

66 On the last point, see Bateson (1972).
67 Although not an explicitly postmodernist text, see Carr (1986).

identified with postmodernism are actually a ritualistic and compromisingly modernist attempt at demystification.[68]

At the very heart of their effect now, both of fantasy in general and Tolkien in particular, is that of wonder. It has been given profound new life by the postmodern cultural project of re-enchantment. Along with Brian Attebery, C.N. Manlove (1983:156) – otherwise no fan of Tolkien – sees this clearly: "there is a very definite and constant character to fantasy, and in nothing is it perhaps so markedly constant as its devotion to wonder at created things, and its profound sense that that wonder is above almost everything else a spiritual good not to be lost."[69]

But critics like Jack Zipes and Marina Warner – despite their pre-eminence on the subject of fantasy, fairy tales and myth – sadly do not. The reason is plain: their subject-matter is less significant than their commitments to cultural materialism and political feminism respectively – projects that take place within the modernist problematic, where that of mythopoeic enchantment (including near-relations like creative 'DIY' politics, eco-feminism and neo-paganism) subverts it.

Three Critics

Let me briefly flesh out this indictment. In Zipes's *Breaking the Spell* (1979), real and exciting insights successfully struggled free of Marxist dogma and turgid academic jargon. Drawing on Marcuse and Bloch, Zipes argued convincingly that

> To the extent that the folk and fairy tales of old as well as the new ones form alternative configurations in a critical and imaginative reflection of the dominant social norms and ideas, they contain an emancipatory *potential* which can never be completely controlled or depleted unless human subjectivity itself is fully computerized and rendered impotent.
> (Zipes 1979:18)

---

68 Cf. Beatie (1967:8): "The more real it seems, the more fictional it is." An instance of the last-mentioned tendency is Calvino's interminable *If on a Winter's Night a Traveller* (in contrast with his own earlier wonderful tales, such as *The Baron in the Trees*.)

69 Cf. Brian Attebery (1980:3).

And he convincingly applied this *aperçu* to Tolkien.

Sadly, his more recent *Fairy Tales as Myth, Myth as Fairy Tale* (1994) marks a retreat to dogma. He (1994:6) approvingly quotes Barthes on myth as really "*nothing but* a product of class division and its moral, cultural and aesthetic consequences". His own definition of myth is any discourse with "a structure, image, metaphor, plot, and value [fixed] as sacrosanct" (Zipes 1994:15).[70] This is one way (political and epistemological) of looking at it, to be sure; but by itself, it is too facile, abstract and (above all) amenable to a modernist appropriation whereby myth in its original meaning becomes cognate with falsehood, delusion and infantilism.[71]

His definition is therefore seriously inadequate (especially for a book nominally half-devoted to the subject). This could be done in a number of ways; in order of generality, for example, Milton Scarborough (1994) suggests convincingly that myth is an orientation for existence which is not only comprehensive of the life-world but a special 'a priori' condition of all theoretical thinking.[72] Less ambitiously, there is myth as culturally collective narratives which help people answer ethical/existential questions, and whose truths therefore surpass properly factual or 'scientific' justification. Or there is Roberto Calasso's suggestion, which has the virtues of historical and cultural specificity, and simplicity: "Stories of the gods and heroes as defined by the ancients."[73] Finally, isn't there a thread running through each of these views?

In any case, we can place no confidence in Zipes as a guide here – not even where the last suggested definition, surely closest in spirit to the other half of his subject-matter, fairy-tales, is concerned. For example, his free-

---

[70] (Emphasis added). Zipes's text is also marred by the worst kind of in-house academic jargon, e.g., "the evolution of the fairy tale as a literary genre is marked by a process of dialectical appropriation involving duplication and revision that set the cultural conditions for its mythicization, institutionalization, and expansion as a mass-mediated form [...]" (Zipes 1994:10).

[71] I am aware, of course, that such a definition has much older roots, notably in that great enemy of myth, Plato.

[72] Cf. Dews (1995), on the unavoidability of metaphysics.

[73] At a talk at the South Bank, London, on 11 November 1995.

association about Robert Bly's title *Iron John* results in twenty-four names and concepts (1994:96). Yet extraordinarily, Mars (or Ares) never occurs to him, although through its 'rulership' of iron, it is precisely the ancient mythical key – from its Mesopotamian roots and Greek and Roman versions, through its Hermetic codification and Renaissance neo-Platonic restatement, to its ubiquitous appearance in modern astrological discourse – to 'Iron John' in all his aspects and symbolic associations (masculinity, hardness, war and so on). As Paracelsus wrote, "He who knows what iron is, knows the attributes of Mars. He who knows Mars, knows the qualities of iron." And he who doesn't, he might have added, knows neither.[74]

Zipes also possesses the usual modernist faith in the power of demystification. (Not that there is anything wrong with faith as such; but with this particular one, yes.) Thus, he seems to think that the chief problem with Disney is that "[t]he pictures conceal the controls and the machinery. They deprive the audience of viewing the production and manipulation, and in the end, audiences can no longer envision a fairy tale for themselves as they can when they read it" (1994:84). The last point is right, but not for the reason he gives. Viewing Disney's production and manipulation involved in making Disney films would interest, let alone 'free', very few people; indeed, it wouldn't work, so to speak, unless it was itself the (successful) result of such a process. Conversely, the pathology of Disney films lies not in production/manipulation – which, as such, is unavoidable – but in the particular *kind* they involve: the true and deliberate infantilizing of imagery, the relentless exploitation of both the medium and the stories for colonizing the imagination, and all driven by the logic of a global pop monoculture, a culture of capital itself, with all its unmatched ability "to degrade, vulgarise, constrict, or, as the argot has it, 'tabloidise'" (Cockburn 1995).

As Tolkien («On Fairy-Stories», 1988:50) said, the creative desire for enchantment "is only cheated by counterfeits, whether the innocent but clumsy devices of the human dramatist, or the malevolent frauds of the

---

74 If I was asked who I trust on the subject, I would include: Walter Otto, Heinrich Zimmer, Karl Kerenyi, Roberto Calasso, P L. Travers, Ursula Le Guin and Tolkien. In other words, it is a necessary if insufficient prerequisite at least to respect myth in its own terms.

magicians" – and with computerized film, these two are as one. But revealing their means of production and manipulation will have negligible effect; if you want to undermine Disney, you must give people (or if you are parents, find) *something better*: in other words, not a disenchantment but an alternative enchantment.[75]

Turning to Marina Warner, one is struck by certain paradoxes. One is that such a prolific author, and one claiming such a wide remit, could omit so much; her recent *From the Beast to the Blonde* (1994), despite the comprehensive sub-title, does not actually concern fairy tales at all, but "traditional nursery classics". Even then, there is no discussion of any such classics featuring boys (*Puss in Boots, Tom Thumb, Jack and the Beanstalk*, etc.), nor the stories of such authors as George MacDonald, Hans Christian Anderson, or Tolkien.[76] (And lest I be accused of merely subjective partisanship, let us recall that *The Hobbit* is easily the most popular fairy story of this century.) The doubt unavoidably stirs that these were simply unamenable to what she wanted to conclude.

Another curious thing, if more ineffable, is the distinct odour of sanctity that clings to this avowedly secular and analytical writer's work – one that noticeably exceeds any attached to that of Tolkien, an unshakable Catholic. The reason, it seems to me, is Warner's devout adherence to the pieties of literary feminism and modernism, acclaimed and protected by the same congregation that has already canonised Angela Carter. Once again, disenchantment and demystification, through revealing the origins of fairy-tales in specific "social and material conditions", is again the secular sacrament.

Another such tenet is the cosy meliorist creed – one of Tolkien's targets in his essay on *Beowulf* – that there is no real, intractable and ultimately irrefragable evil, because (in Warner's words) "monsters are

---

75 Incidentally, the film *Company of Wolves*, based on Angela Carter's disenchanted version of *Red Riding Hood*, provides a perfect example; although its director, Neil Jordan, was at least as responsible as she for the extent to which it bears out Tolkien's pessimism. Films that enchant are possible, if rare.

76 The same was true of another ambitiously-entitled address, «Re-Thinking the Uses of Enchantment», on 21 June 1992, at The Society of Antiquaries of London.

made, not given. And if monsters are made, they can be unmade, too" (*The Independent*, 3.2.94).[77] Thus, interviewed about the recent slaughter of Scottish school-children, she delicately eschews 'evil' for 'vice'; even when confronted with the example of Nazism, she will not look it in the eye, proferring instead that "I don't think there was enough resistance there. People were duped or taken in and the vitiation spread [...]" (quoted in Porter 1996).

Vitiation! This is a serious failure of the moral imagination – as if, to quote Le Guin (1989:58-59),

> evil were a problem, something that can be solved, that has an answer, like a problem in fifth grade arithmetic. [...] *That* is escapism, that posing evil as a 'problem', instead of what it is: all the pain and suffering and waste and loss and injustice we will meet all our lives long, and must face and cope with over and over, and admit, and live with, in order to live human lives at all.

That, as we have seen, was Tolkien's opinion too.

Finally, a genteel but relentless concern with the single dimension of gender excludes everything that is not grist to its mill; thus, any hint of the power of myth, folk- and fairy-tales to induce wonder *as such* – the very heart, in a postmodern context, of Tolkien's («On Fairy-Stories», 1988:32) "point too often forgotten: that is the effect produced *now* by these old things in the stories as they are" – is utterly absent. She thus misses an invaluable opportunity to counter the stranglehold of a schlerotic modernism on literature and criticism, one of the chief remedies for which is precisely, in Ihab Hassan's (1992:204) words, "to remythify the imagination, at least locally, and bring back the reign of wonder into our lives."

Once again, unsung readers probably have the edge on literary professionals. The great Indologist Heinrich Zimmer pointed to the heart of the matter:

---

77 Cf. "Children are our copy, in little [...]" (*The Independent*, 10.2.94).

> The dilettante – Italian 'dilettante' (present participle of the verb 'dilettare', 'to take delight in') – is one who takes delight in something. [...] The moment we abandon this dilettante attitude toward the images of folklore and myth and begin to feel certain about their proper interpretation (as professional comprehenders, handling the tool of an infallible method), we deprive ourselves of the quickening contact, the demonic and inspiring assault that is the effect of their intrinsic virtue. We forfeit our proper humility and open-mindedness before the unknown, and refuse to be instructed. [...] What they demand of us is not the monologue of the coroner's report, but the dialogue of a living conversation.
> (Zimmer 1948:1-3)

Jameson's "Magical Narratives"

There is no better example of the coroner's report than my third choice of critic Frederic Jameson's «Magical Narratives: Romance as Genre», so I am going to give it a little extra attention. It was published in 1975, and many of its premises (notably the Marxist metaphysics) have suffered since then. But many of Jameson's generation who shared his convictions are now ensconsed in positions of institutional power. And as his subsequent work shows, the fundamentals of those convictions have changed little; his subsequent 'post-modernism' is really simply neo-Marxism, in which the command "Always historicize" applies to everything except itself and its own particular assumptions.

Discussing Vladimir Propp's structuralist analysis of folktales as "a process of abstraction, whereby *surface* events or elements are assimilated to emptier and ever more general categories", Jameson criticizes it as insufficiently coronistic – or in his words, "still too meaningful". He wants "a type of analysis which aims at seeing the entire narrative in terms of a single [...] *mechanism*" (Jameson 1975:146-48; my emphases). What better statement of the modernist dream, with its chilling monist and imperialist ambitions, could be imagined?

Along the way, so-called "surface events" are not the only victims. So too is "the belief in good and evil" – apparently *any* kind of such belief. This fundamental human experience is dismissed as "a magical thought mode, that is, one which springs from a precapitalist, essentially agricultural way of life" (Jameson 1975:141). And since the mode of production is all-powerful, the reader

> now finds himself obliged to justify the henceforth scandalous and archaic activity of fantasy, so that what we have called the replacements for the older magical function also serve as so many rational ways of explaining it away – in Stendhal by way of psychology, and in Eichendorff by the demonstration that it was not really there at all in the first place.
> (Jameson 1975:145)

We must ask: really? Are there any of these modernist "replacements" in *The Lord of the Rings*? And do any of its millions of readers miss them?

Perhaps that is why Jameson (1975:161) specifies the work of Tolkien and Lewis as "archaic nostalgia" (which, for modernists, is about the worst thing you can say). But his own theory cannot explain either their continued existence or popularity except as pure mass infantilism, which really ought (or should it be, who ought?) to be eliminated. The higher knowledge/cause that justifies this lofty purism is our old friend Marx and Engel's "base": that muscular starting point of 'real men' and 'real existence' which consigns to the dustbin of epiphenomena "what men say, imagine, conceive [...] men as narrated, thought of, imagined, conceived. [...] Morality, religion, metaphysics, all the rest of ideology and their corresponding forms of consciousness". Magically enough, the "base" determines all this "superstructure" without being affected in return. And Marxists like Jameson *know* this because their creed is not "simply one more critical language or method among others"; uniquely, its critical operation "requires us to correlate literary phenomena, not with [...] conceptual abstractions, but rather with the realities to which those abstractions correspond" (1975:157, 159). That is, Marxist concepts alone, being somehow not conceptual, escape abstraction. Such an assertion has all the intellectual authority of 'what I tell you three times is true'.[78]

For many readers, this will be old ground, hardly worth retracing. But I disagree; we need reminding of the arrogant fatuity that has become a mentality, an entrenched habit of thought amounting to a 'déformation professionelle', among many influential literary professionals. This is what anyone who wants to see understanding (as well as explanation) and value (as well as interpretation) restored to the heart of the critical enterprise is up against. Such a reader might well take heart from the rich perceptiveness – the wisdom, to give it its proper name – of Walter Benjamin, who lamented the dying out of "the epic side of truth, wisdom" (1969:89), and with it, the art of storytelling:

> no event any longer comes to us without already being shot through with explanation. In other words, by now almost nothing that happens benefits storytelling; almost everything benefits information. Actually, it is half the art of storytelling to keep a story free from explanation as one reproduces it. [...] There is nothing that commends a story to memory more effectively than that chaste compactness which precludes psychological analysis.
> (Benjamin 1969:91)

Benjamin concludes, in words that apply directly to Tolkien and celebrate the survival of what Jameson regards as an atavistic abberation, that "The first true storyteller is, *and will continue to be*, the teller of fairy tales" (1969:102).

Three Writers

The approach I have urged has interesting implications for various writers, too – especially those who apparently share the category of 'fantasy', and draw on the same stock of myth, folk- and fairy-tales. Here, very briefly, are three examples. The stories of Terry Pratchett, the hugely successful English comic fantasy writer, are stuffed with trolls, dwarves, witches and wizards

---

[78] Thompson's wonderful polemic (1978) is still relevant here.

and magic generally. Yet these are devices he uses to produce quintessentially humanist tales. But not of the scientific and universalist modernist kind – Pratchett's idiom is unmistakably local, *i.e.* English (not 'British'), and his humanism is in the best pre-modern Montaignian tradition of humane, tolerant, sceptical humanism. In Elgin's terms, Pratchett is a comic and ecological writer: accepting of nature, the body, and human limits.[79] As such, his stories partake of postmodern localism and pluralism; and they refresh, not dessicate, the contemporary soul.

My second example is the vivid contrast between Tolkien's work and that of the late Angela Carter. This goes deeper than the latter's earthy feminism, and the generation gap between her 1960s anti-authoritarianism and Tolkien's residually Edwardian love of a quiet, green world. Consider the fact that Carter's best fiction centres on the circus and the theatre, both arenas whose magic, while potent, falls well within the humanist and secular ambit of drama. This is an art-form which, if Tolkien was right, is necessarily anthropocentric, unlike literature, which can (if rarely now does) escape into the non-human world, or nature – and thus nature, in turn, into art. And literature which harkens back to ancient myth would have a special impetus, and ability, to let the voices of non-human nature speak.

True, the two authors drew upon many of the same European and English folk- and fairy-tales; and Alison Lurie (1996) thinks Carter shares a Northern air with Karen Blixen that I had already decided linked the latter with Tolkien. But I would contend that their projects were exactly opposite; Carter was primarily interested in *dis*enchanting her readers – freeing them from a false glamour cast by a sexist and racist capitalism – whereas he, despite sharing to a surprising extent the same concerns, was trying to work an alternative *re*-enchantment.

These represent very different strategies. Neither is necessarily more effective than the other; Carter's sophisticated and anti-mythic subversion of enchantment limits her audience in one way, just as Tolkien's contrary approach does his in another. In terms of appeal discernible through sheer

---

79 In this as well as in narrower literary terms, the comparison with P.G. Wodehouse is not misplaced.

numbers of readers, of course, Tolkien obviously has the edge. But I would also reject the suggestion that Carter's left-of-centre affiliations notwithstanding, her work is inherently more 'radical'. Indeed, if I am right about the destructiveness of unchecked modernity, then Tolkien's is the more needed; and, ironically, the less naive. (The same could be said of Fay Weldon's fiction, for example, and Warner's criticism; but definitely not of the work of Ursula Le Guin – surely no less a feminist than they, so that cannot be the fundamental consideration.)

Nor, in my terms, is Salman Rushdie, my third example, a consistently or successfully postmodern writer. For all its irony, pastiche and hybridity, *The Satanic Verses* was correctly recognized by its Asian Islamic readers (for all their near-illiteracy) as a serious secularist attack on their religion: a classic case of modernist debunking, in fact.[80] And it is significant that both Carter and Rushdie – the former rightly praised by the latter as "a thumber of noses, a defiler of sacred cows" – have declared their devotion to *The Wizard of Oz*.[81] For the fundamental point about the Wizard of Oz – Oz the Great and Terrible – is this: he was a cheat and a fraud, and as such, a comforting anti-fairy-tale for secular and modernist Grown-Ups: just "a little, old man, with a bald head and a wrinkled face". "'Hush, my dear [...] don't speak so loud, or you will be overheard – and I should be ruined. I'm supposed to be a Great Wizard.' 'And aren't you?' [...] 'Not a bit of it, my dear; I'm just a common man'" (Baum 1993:122-23).

Now if I were ('horribile dictu') Fred Inglis, I would now play my trump card, and point out that while it would be disgraceful to use the fact against him, it should nonetheless be noted that L. Frank Baum was a violent racist who publicly advocated genocide against the (remaining) American Indians.[82] I will content myself, however, with noting that Baum doesn't exactly leave Tolkien gasping at the back of the radical sweepstakes; and since reactionary modernists abound (Wyndham Lewis,

---

80 This should not, of course, be taken to imply that I agree in the slightest with the outrageous 'fatwa' threatening his life.
81 *New York Times Book Review* (8.3.92),
82 See *Twin Light Trail: American Indian News* 2 (1992):15.

T.S. Eliot, and many Weimar intellectuals),[83] so political backwardness, too, cannot really be the problem.

The real problem Tolkien poses for modernists is that his work has committed the crime – like a felled tree he once mourned – of being "large and alive." Its success calls time on them, and underscores their own dead hand. And not before time. For wonder alone cannot save us, or a world worth living in; but without it, the outlook is very dark indeed.[84]

PATRICK CURRY is Canadian-born but lives in London, England. He has a Ph.D. from the University of London in the history and philosophy of science. He is the author of two books of social history (and editor of one), as well as *Machiavelli for Beginners* (1995) and *Defending Middle Earth: Tolkien, Myth and Modernity* (1997, HarperCollins paperback edition 1998; American paperback edition by Houghton Mifflin 2004). He is senior lecturer at the Sophia Centre, Bath Spa University College.

---

83 See Herf (1984), Harrison (1966), and Carey (1992).
84 See the superb analysis by Hepburn (1984), which I have used in Curry (1999).

References

ACACELLA, Joan. 1995. «Cather and the Academy.» *The New Yorker* (27.11.1995):57-71.

ATTEBERY, Brian. 1980. *The Fantasy Tradition in American Literature*. Bloomington: Indiana University Press.

- - -. 1992. *Strategies of Fantasy*. Bloomington: Indiana University Press.

BARFIELD, Owen. 1977. «The Meaning of 'Literal'.» In: *The Rediscovery of Meaning, and Other Essays*. Middletown CT: Wesleyan University Press, 32-43.

BARRELL, John and John BULL (eds.). 1974. *The Penguin Book of English Pastoral Verse*. Harmondsworth: Penguin.

BATE, Jonathan. 1991. *Romantic Ecology: Wordsworth and the Environmental Tradition*. London: Routledge.

BATESON, Gregory. 1972. *Steps to an Ecology of Mind*. New York: Chandler/Ballantine Books.

BAUM, Frank L. 1993. *The Wizard of Oz*. Ware, Herts.: Wordsworth Editions. 1st edition c. 1900.

BAUMAN, Zygmunt. 1989. *Modernity and the Holocaust*. Cambridge: Polity Press.

- - -. 1992. *Intimations of Postmodernity*. London: Routledge.

BEATIE, Bruce A. 1967. «Folk Tale, Fiction, and Saga in J.R.R. Tolkien's *Lord of the Rings*.» *The Tolkien Papers Mankato State College Studies* II.1:1-17.

BENJAMIN, Walter. 1969. «The Storyteller» In: *Illuminations: Essays and Reflections*. Edited by Hannah ARENDT. New York: Schocken Books, 83-109.

BERNSTEIN, Jay. 1996. «The Death of Sensuous Particulars: Adorno and Abstract Expressionism.» *Radical Philosophy* 76:7-18.

BJORGO, Tore (ed.). 1995. *Terror from the Extreme Right*. London: Frank Cass.

BRANSTON, Brian. 1957. *The Lost Gods of England*. London: Thames and Hudson.

BROOKE-ROSE, Christine. 1980. «The Evil Ring: Realism and the Marvellous.» *Poetics Today* 1.4: 67-90.

- - -. 1981. *A Rhetoric of the Unreal: Studies in Narrative and Structure, Especially of the Fantastic*. Cambridge: Cambridge University Press.

BUFORD, Bill. 1996. «The Seductions of Storytelling.» *The New Yorker* (24.6 & 1.7.96):11-12.

BURKE, Kenneth. 1957. *Counter-Statement*. 2nd edition. 1st edition 1953. Chicago: University of Chicago Press.

BUTLER, Hubert. 1986. *Escape from the Anthill*. Mullingar: Lilliput Press.

CAREY, John. 1977. «Hobbit-Forming.» *The Listener* (12.5.1977):631.

- - -. 1992. *The Intellectuals and the Masses*. London: Faber.

CARPENTER, Humphrey. 1992. *Tolkien: A Biography*. First published 1977. London: Grafton.

CARR, David. 1986. *Time, Narrative and History*. Bloomington: Indiana University Press.

COCKBURN, Alexander. 1995. «Fatal Attraction.» *The Guardian* (12.5.1995).

COLEBATCH, Hal. 1990. *Return of the Heroes. The Lord of the Rings, Star Wars and Contemporary Culture*. Perth: Australian Institute for Public Policy.

CRAIG, Amanda. 1992. «Lord of All He Conveyed, Despite His Fans.» *The Independent* (25.1.1992).

CUNNINGHAM, Valentine. 1989. *British Writers of the Thirties*. Oxford: Oxford University Press.

CURRY, Patrick. 1995. *Machiavelli for Beginners*. Cambridge: Icon Books.

- - -. 1997. *Defending Middle-Earth: Tolkien, Myth and Modernity*. Edinburgh: Floris Books, New York: St Martin's Press; paperback edition 1998, London: HarperCollins.

- - -. 1999. «Magic vs. Enchantment.» Journal of Contemporary Religion 14.3:401-412.

DAVIE, Donald. 1973. *Thomas Hardy and British Poetry*. London: Routledge and Kegan Paul.

DERRIDA, Jacques. 1988. «Afterword: Toward an Ethic of Discussion.» In: *Limited Inc*. Evanston: Northwestern University Press, 111-60.

- - -. 1994. *Spectres of Marx*. London: Verso.

DEWS, Peter. 1995. *The Limits of Disenchantment*. London: Verso.

DODDS, David Llewellyn. 1993-94. «The Centrality of Sex in Middle-Earth.» *Lembas Extra* (1993-94):59-80.

DRABBLE, Margaret. 1985. *The Oxford Companion to English Literature*. Oxford: Oxford University Press.

- - - and Jenny STRINGER. 1996. *Oxford Concise Companion to English Literature*. Oxford: Oxford University Press.

EASTHOPE, Anthony. 1991. *Literary into Cultural Studies*. London: Routledge.

EHRENFIELD, David. 1978. *The Arrogance of Humanism*. Oxford: Oxford University Press.

- - -. 1993. «The Roots of Prophecy: Orwell and Nature.» In: *Beginning Again: People and Nature in the New Millenium*. Oxford: Oxford University Press, 8-28.

EKINS, Paul. 1992. *A New World Order: Grassroots Movements for Global Change*. London: Routledge.

ELGIN, Don R. 1985. *The Comedy of the Fantastic. Ecological Perspectives on the Fantasy Novel*. Westport: The Greenwood Press.

EMPSON, William. 1979. *Some Versions of Pastoral*. London: Chatto & Windus.

ENDE, Michael. 1993. *The Never-Ending Story*. English translation of *Die unendliche Geschichte*, originally published 1979. London: Roc/Penguin.

EWIJCK, Annemarie van. 1995. «Sex in Middle-Earth.» *Lembas Extra* (1995):23-33.

EZARD, John. 1991. «Tolkien's Shire.» *The Guardian* (28-29.12.91).

FELPERIN, Howard. 1985. *Beyond Deconstruction: The Uses and Abuses of Literary Theory*. Oxford: Clarendon Press.

FEYERABEND, Paul. 1987. *Farewell to Reason*. London: Verso.

FILMER, Kath. 1992. *Scepticism and Hope in Twentieth Century Fantasy Literature*. Bowling Green: Bowling Green State University Popular Press.

FINCH, Jason. 1994. «Democratic Government in Middle-earth.» *Amon Hen* 129:12-13.

FLIEGER, Verlyn. 1983. *Splintered Light: Logos and Language in Tolkien's World*. Grand Rapids: Wm. Eerdmans.

GIDDINGS, Robert (ed.). 1983. *J.R.R. Tolkien: This Far Land*. London: Vision Press.

- - - and Elizabeth HOLLAND. 1981. *J.R.R. Tolkien: The Shores of Middle-earth*. London: Junction Books.

GOLDTHWAITE, John. 1996. *The Natural History of Make-Believe: A Guide to the Principal Works of Britain, Europe and America*. Oxford: Oxford University Press.

GOPNIK, Adam. 1994. «Grim Fairy Tales.» *The New Yorker* (12.12.94):84-102.

GRANT, Patrick. 1981. «Tolkien: Archetype and Word.» In: ISAACS, Neil D. and Rose A. ZIMBARDO. (eds.). 1981. *Tolkien: New Critical Perspectives*. Lexington: University of Kentucky Press, 87-105.

GRAY, John. 1995. *Enlightenment's Wake: Politics and Culture at the Close of the Modern Age*. London: Routledge.

GRIGORIEVA, Natalia. 1995. «Problems of Translation into Russian.» In: REYNOLDS, Patricia and Glen H. GOODKNIGHT (eds.). 1995. *Proceedings of the J.R.R. Tolkien Centenary Conference*. Milton Keynes: The Tolkien Society / Altadena: The Mythopoeic Press, 200-205.

GRUSHETSKIY, Vladimir. 1995. «How Russians See Tolkien.» In: REYNOLDS, Patricia and Glen H. GOODKNIGHT (eds.). 1995. *Proceedings of the J.R.R. Tolkien Centenary Conference*. Milton Keynes: The Tolkien Society / Altadena: The Mythopoeic Press, 221-225.

HAMMOND, Wayne G. 1995. «The Critical Response to Tolkien's Fiction.» In: REYNOLDS, Patricia and Glen H. GOODKNIGHT (eds.). 1995. *Proceedings of the J.R.R. Tolkien Centenary Conference*. Milton Keynes: The Tolkien Society / Altadena: The Mythopoeic Press, 226-32.

HARRISON, Fraser. 1984. «England, Home and Beauty.» In: MABEY, Richard with Susan CLIFFORD and Angela KING (eds.). 1984. *Second Nature*. London: Jonathan Cape, 162-72.

HARRISON, John R. 1966. *The Reactionaries*. London: Victor Gollancz.

HARRISON, Robert Pogue. 1992. *Forests: The Shadow of Civilization*. Chicago: University of Chicago Press.

HASSAN, Ihab. 1992 «Pluralism in Postmodern Perspective.» In: JENCKS, Charles (ed.). 1992. *The Post-Modern Reader*. London: Academy Editions, 196-207.

HEPBURN, Ronald. 1984. *'Wonder' and other Essays*. Edinburgh: Edinburgh University Press.

HERBERT, Kathleen. 1993. *Spellcraft: Old English Heroic Legends*. Hockwold-cum-Wilton, Norfolk: Anglo-Saxon Books.

HERF, Jeffrey. 1984. *Reactionary Modernism*. Cambridge: Cambridge University Press.

HIPOLITO, T.A. 1993. «Owen Barfield's Poetic Diction.» *Renascence* 46.1:3-38.

HITCHENS, Christopher. 1993. «Something about the Poetry: Larkins and 'Sensitivity'.» *New Left Review* 200:161-74.

- - -. 1994. «Dr Strangelove, I presume?» *New Statesman and Society* (30.9.94):44-45.

HOBAN, Russell. 1992. *The Moment Under the Moment*. London: Jonathan Cape.

HUGHES, Ted. 1992. *The Goddess of Complete Being*. London: Faber.

HUYSSEN, Andreas. 1986. *After the Great Divide: Modernism, Mass Culture, Postmodernism*. London: Macmillan Press.

INGLIS, Fred. 1981. *The Promise of Happiness: Value and Meaning in Children's Fiction.* Cambridge: Cambridge University Press.

- - -. 1983. «Gentility and Powerlessness: Tolkien and the New Class.» In: GIDDINGS, Robert (ed.). 1983. *J.R.R. Tolkien: This Far Land.* London: Vision Press, 25-41.

- - -. 1994. *Cultural Studies.* Oxford: Basil Blackwell.

- - -. 1995. *Raymond Williams.* London: Routledge.

ISAACS, Neil D. and Rose A. ZIMBARDO (eds.). 1968. *Tolkien and the Critics.* Notre Dame: University of Notre Dame Press.

- - - and Rose A. ZIMBARDO (eds.). 1981. *Tolkien: New Critical Perspectives.* Lexington: University of Kentucky Press.

JACKSON, Rosemary. 1988. *Fantasy: The Literature of Subversion.* London: Routledge.

JAMESON, Frederic. 1975. «Magical Narratives: Romance as Genre.» *New Literary History* 7.1:135-63.

JOHANNESSON, Nils-Lennart. 1997. «The Speech of the Individual and of the Community in The Lord of the Rings.» In: BUCHS, Peter and Thomas HONEGGER (eds.). 1997. *News from the Shire and Beyond – Studies on Tolkien.* Zurich and Berne: Walking Tree Publishers, 12-47.

JOHNSON, Judith A. 1986. *J.R.R. Tolkien: Six Decades of Criticism.* Bibliographies and Indexes in World Literature 6. Westport, CT: Greenwood Press.

KAMENKOVICH, Maria. 1992. «The Secret War and the End of the First Age: Tolkien in the (former) USSR.» *Mallorn* 29:33-38.

KAVENEY, Roz. 1991. «The Ring Recycled.» *New Statesman and Society* (20 & 27.12.1991).

KEARNEY, Richard. 1985. «Myth and Motherland.» In: DEANE, Seamus et al. 1985. *Ireland's Field Day.* London: Hutchinson, 61-80.

KILBY, Clyde. 1977. *Tolkien and the Silmarillion.* Berkhamsted: Lion Publishing.

KOLAKOWSKI, Leszek. 1990. *Modernity on Endless Trial.* Chicago: University of Chicago Press.

KONTOS, Alkis. 1994. «The World Disenchanted, and the Return of Gods and Demons.» In: HOROWITZ, Asher and Terry MALEY (eds.). *The Barbarism of Reason: Max Weber and the Twilight of the Enlightenment.* Toronto: University of Toronto Press, 223-247.

LACLAU, Ernesto and Chantal MOUFFE. 1985. *Hegemony and Socialist Strategy. Toward a Radical Democratic Politics.* London: Verso.

LE GUIN, Ursula K. 1989. *The Languages of the Night.* Edited by Susan Wood. London: The Woman's Press. (1st edition 1979. New York: Berkeley Books.)

LEVI, Primo. 1987. *If This Is A Man and The Truce.* London: Sphere Books.

LOBDELL, Jared (ed.). 1975. *A Tolkien Compass.* La Salle: Open Court.

LUCAS, John. 1990. *England and Englishness.* London: Hogarth Press.

LULING, Virginia. 1995. «An Anthropologist in Middle-earth.» In: REYNOLDS, Patricia and Glen H. GOODKNIGHT (eds.). 1995. *Proceedings of the J.R.R. Tolkien Centenary Conference.* Milton Keynes: The Tolkien Society / Altadena: The Mythopoeic Press, 53-57.

LURIE, Alison. 1990. *Don't Tell the Grown-Ups. Subversive Children's Literature.* London: Bloomsbury.

- - -. 1996. «Winter's Tales.» *The N.Y. Times Book Review* (19.5.1996).

MANLOVE, C.N. 1983. *The Impulse of Fantasy Literature*. London: Macmillan.

MCLEISH, Kenneth. 1983. «The Rippingest Yarn of All.» In: GIDDINGS, Robert (ed.). 1983. *J.R.R. Tolkien: This Far Land*. London: Vision Press, 125-36.

MEYERS, Jeffrey. 1995. *Edmund Wilson*. London: Constable.

MIDGELEY, Mary. 1997. «Sneer Tactics.» *The Guardian* (7.9.97).

MOORCOCK, Michael. 1987. *Wizardry and Wild Romance*. London: Victor Gollancz.

MUIRHEAD, Ian A. 1986. «Theology in Gandalf's Garden.» *Arda* (1986):14-24.

NICHOLSON-LORD, David. 1995. «Write Me a Novel I Can Actually Read.» *The Independent on Sunday* (30.4.95).

O'CONNOR, Alan. 1989. *Raymond Williams: Writing, Culture, Politics*. Oxford: Basil Blackwell.

OTTY, Nick. 1983. «A Structuralist's Guide to Middle-Earth.» In: GIDDINGS, Robert (ed.). 1983. *J.R.R. Tolkien: This Far Land*. London: Vision Press, 154-78.

PARK, James. 1991. *Cultural Icons*. London: Bloomsbury.

PARKER, Douglass. 1956-57. «Hwaet We Holbytla...» *The Hudson Review* 9.4:598-609.

PARTRIDGE, Brenda. 1983. «No Sex Please – We're Hobbits: The Construction of Female Sexuality in *The Lord of the Rings*.» In: GIDDINGS, Robert (ed.). 1983. *J.R.R. Tolkien: This Far Land*. London: Vision Press, 179-97.

PAYNE, Stanley G. 1996. *A History of Fascism, 1914-1945*. Madison: University of Wisconsin Press.

PLANK, Robert. 1975. «The Scouring of the Shire: Tolkien's View of Fascism.» In: LOBDELL, Jared (ed.). 1975. *A Tolkien Compass*. La Salle: Open Court, 107-15.

PORTER, Henry. 1996. «Reason Eclipsed by Evil.» *The Guardian* (17.3.1996).

POTTER, Dennis. 1984. *Waiting for the Boat: On Television*. London: Faber & Faber.

RAFFEL, Burton. 1968. «*The Lord of the Rings* as Literature.» In: ISAACS, Neil D. and Rose A. ZIMBARDO (eds.). 1968. *Tolkien and the Critics*. Notre Dame: University of Notre Dame Press, 218-46.

REYNOLDS, Patricia and Glen H. GOODKNIGHT (eds.). 1995. *Proceedings of the J.R.R. Tolkien Centenary Conference*. Milton Keynes: The Tolkien Society / Altadena: The Mythopoeic Press.

ROSEBURY, Brian. 1992. *Tolkien: A Critical Assessment*. London: Macmillan Press.

SAMUEL, Raphael. 1995. *Theatres of Memory*. London: Verso.

SAUNDERS, Andrew. 1994. *The Short Oxford History of English Literature*. Oxford: Oxford University Press.

SCARBOROUGH, Milton. 1994. *Myth and Modernity: Postcritical Reflections*. Albany: SUNY Press.

SCHEPPS, Walter. 1975. «The Fairy-tale Morality of *The Lord of the Rings*.» In: LOBDELL, Jared (ed.). 1975. *A Tolkien Compass*. La Salle: Open Court, 43-56.

SCHNADELBACH, Herbert. 1992. «The Face in the Sand: Foucault and the Anthropological Slumber.» In: HONNETH, Axel et al. (eds.). *Philosophical Interventions in the Unfinished Project of Enlightenment*. Cambridge, MA: Harvard University Press.

SHIPPEY, T.A. 1992. *The Road to Middle-Earth*. 2nd edition. 1st edition 1982. London: Grafton/HarperCollins.

- - -. 1995. «Tolkien as a Post-War Writer.» In: REYNOLDS, Patricia and Glen H. GOODKNIGHT (eds.). 1995. *Proceedings of the J.R.R. Tolkien Centenary Conference*. Milton Keynes: The Tolkien Society / Altadena: The Mythopoeic Press, 84-93.

- - -. 1996. «Burbocentrism.» *London Review of Books* (23.5.1996).

SMITH, Barbara Herrnstein. 1988. *Contingencies of Value: Alternative Perspectives for Critical Theory*. Cambridge, MA: Harvard University Press.

STIMPSON, Catherine R. 1969. *J.R.R. Tolkien*. Columbia Essays on Modern Writers 41. New York: Columbia University Press.

STRINGER, Jenny (ed.). 1996. *The Oxford Companion to Twentieth-Century Literature in English*. Oxford: Oxford University Press.

SWINFEN, Ann. 1984. *In Defence of Fantasy. A Study of the Genre in English and American Literature since 1945*. London: Routledge Kegan Paul.

THOMPSON, E.P.1976. *William Morris*. 2nd edition. 1st edition 1955. New York: Pantheon.

- - -. 1978. *The Poverty of Theory and Other Essays*. London: Merlin Press.

- - -. 1993. *Witness Against the Beast: William Blake and the Moral Law*. Cambridge: Cambridge University Press.

TIMMONS, Daniel. 1996. «J.R.R. Tolkien's Genealogies: The Roots of His 'Sub-creation'.» *Mallorn* 34:7-11.

TOLKIEN, J.R.R. 1981. *The Letters of J.R.R. Tolkien*. Edited by Humphrey CARPENTER. London: George, Allen and Unwin.

- - -. 1988. «On Fairy-Stories.» In: *Tree and Leaf*. London: Unwin Hyman. (The original essay was first delivered as a lecture in 1939, and first published, somewhat enlarged, in 1947.)

- - -. 1991. *The Lord of the Rings*. 1st edition 1954-55. London: Grafton/HarperCollins.

TOULMIN, Stephen. 1990. *Cosmopolis. The Hidden Agenda of Modernity*. Chicago: University of Chicago Press.

TURNER, Jenny. 1996. «Lost in the Bush.» Review of Alan Garner's *Strandloper* in *The Guardian* (24.5.1996).

VELDMAN, Meredith. 1994. *Fantasy, the Bomb, and the Greening of Britain: Romantic Protest, 1945-1980*. Cambridge: Cambridge University Press.

VEYNE, Paul. 1988. *Did the Greeks Believe Their Myths?* English translation. Originally published 1983. Chicago: University of Chicago Press.

WALMSLEY, Nigel. 1983. «Tolkien and the '60s.» In: GIDDINGS, Robert (ed.). 1983. *J.R.R. Tolkien: This Far Land*. London: Vision Press, 73-85.

WEBSTER, Charles. 1982. *From Paracelsus to Newton*. Cambridge: Cambridge University Press.

WEST, R.C. 1970. *Tolkien Criticism: An Annotated Checklist*. Kent: Kent State University Press.

WILLIAMS, Madawc. 1995. «Good Government in Middle-earth.» *Amon Hen* 132:17-19.

WILLIAMS, Raymond. 1985. *The Country and the City*. London: Hogarth Press.

WILMER, Clive (ed.). 1985. *John Ruskin: Unto This Last and Other Writings*. London: Penguin Books.

WILSON, Colin. 1974. *Tree by Tolkien*. Santa Barbara: Capra Press.

WILSON, Edmund. 1956. «Oo, Those Awful Orcs!» *The Nation* 182.15 (14.4.1956):312-14; reprinted in his *The Bit Between my Teeth*. New York: W.H. Allen, 326-32.

WRIGHT, Patrick. 1986. *On Living in an Old Country*. London: Verso.

YATES, Jessica. 1995. «Tolkien the Anti-Totalitarian.» In: REYNOLDS, Patricia and Glen H. GOODKNIGHT (eds.). 1995. *Proceedings of the J.R.R. Tolkien Centenary Conference*. Milton Keynes: The Tolkien Society / Altadena: The Mythopoeic Press, 233-45.

ZIMMER, Heinrich. 1948. *The King and the Corpse. Tales of the Soul's Conquest of Evil*. Princeton: Princeton University Press.

ZIPES, Jack. 1979. *Breaking the Magic Spell: Radical Theories of Folk and Fairy Tales*. London: Heinemann.

- - -. 1994. *Fairy Tale as Myth, Myth as Fairy Tale*. Lexington: The University Press of Kentucky.

Re-enchanting Nature: Some Magic Links between Margaret Atwood and J.R.R. Tolkien

CHRISTINA LJUNGBERG

Summary

Although, at first sight, Margaret Atwood and J.R.R. Tolkien would seem to have little in common, a closer look reveals some intriguing affinities. Both writers use classical and popular mythologies to discuss issues of fundamental human concern; elements of the fantastic appear throughout their narratives, and both endow their characters with archetypal traits. Atwood's investigation of the metaphysical nature of *The Lord of the Rings* in her PhD thesis where she fits it into the English tradition of the metaphysical romance offers interesting insights into the works of both authors.

At first glance, the combination of Margaret Atwood and J.R.R. Tolkien would appear an odd one indeed. Atwood, an astute chronicler of Canadian and, especially, Torontonian fads and fashions, is well known for her commitment to contemporary moral and political issues. In particular, her fictional worlds concern themselves with questions of gender and equality, from a woman writer's perspective. Her distinct witty, self-ironic, morally and politically engaged voice, her acute power of observation and her ability to recreate 'realistic' fictional worlds have had her pigeon-holed as a feminist, post-colonialist, political, or post-modernist writer, among other epithets. That would seem a radical enough contrast to Tolkien's romantic, mainly male fictional universe, where great battles are fought in distant times and places. And, although both writers use classical and popular mythologies to discuss issues of fundamental human concern, Atwood constantly draws attention to their ideological character by reshaping and rewriting them from her own point of view – at the same time as she sprinkles elements of the fantastic throughout her seemingly 'realist' narratives and, like Tolkien, frequently endows her characters with archetypal traits that can be traced back to these mythologies. There is yet another interesting link between the two writers, namely the extent to which two major nexus of ideas occupy central positions in their works: questions of Nature, and of power.

Atwood is often associated with Canadian land. On the one hand, because of her own well publicized childhood in the Canadian wilderness where her father, an entomologist, was conducting field research, and, on the other, because questions of Nature have always been prevalent in Canadian literature, to the point that the Canadian wilderness has become one of the country's most popular myths. This is partly for natural reasons: while the heartland of the neighboring United States is one of the world's most fertile regions, Canada consists of one of the "most ancient wildernesses and one of nature's grimmest challenges to man and all his works," as the Canadian historian W. L. Morton (1972:4-5) puts it. The famous Canadian critic and theorist Northrop Frye (1971:226) is of a similar opinion: he sees the prevalence of Nature and Nature myths in Canadian literature as a result of the difficult and barely penetrable geography that met European traders and settlers when they finally reached the Canadian east coast. In contrast to the steadily westward-moving American frontier, the European travelers entering Canada via the Gulf of St. Lawrence were 'engulfed' by the wilderness, whose frontier "was all around one, a part and a condition of one's whole imaginative being." In Canadian mythology, Nature is therefore often portrayed as something fearful and seen only in negative terms, as a 'disorder' that upsets the cultured environment, a space outside the social order and Christian morals. But, at the same time, Nature also means freedom from the constraints of social rules and regulations, which has resulted in a strangely ambivalent 'double vision' of the wilderness in Canadian literature.

This duplicitous view of Nature is one of the principal themes in Atwood's work in which she frequently turns the natural topography into an enchanted realm in which magical and mysterious transformations take place. Already *The Circle Game* (1966), her first cycle of poems, and the subsequent *The Animals in That Country* (1968), and *Procedures for*

Underground (1970) include poems that in some way or other refer to the land and emphasize the importance of Nature. Geographic orientation becomes the metaphor for orienting oneself in a literary text, in order to inhabit its topography. An interesting case in point is the famous poem opening *The Circle Game*, «This is a photograph of me» (1966/1978:17), which precisely addresses the problems of orientation and interpretation involved in the reading process. In this particular poem – which could easily be read programmatically – geography is taken as a point of departure for an exploration into the reading process as a textual narrative journey through a landscape that is simultaneously exterior and interior. This strategy allows Atwood to create a magical, dynamic space which corresponds to the one between reader, text and the world (see Ljungberg 2001:357).[1]

Atwood's self-reflexive use of Nature to both lay bare what Ronald B. Hatch calls a "landscape of language" (2000:181) and to re-enchant this textual geography forms, I would suggest, an interesting link between Tolkien and Atwood. Tolkien has repeatedly pointed out the importance of language in his work, in which he seeks to inhabit old Celtic and Norse languages and worlds in order to come to terms with modern life. This becomes obvious in his use of historical linguistics and its literatures to recreate cultural myths and histories: there is much in *The Lord of the Rings* that leads one directly to both the Grimm's *Fairy Tales* or the Elder Edda's *Voluspa*, the Icelandic creation myth (cf. Shippey 2000). As is well known, Grimm's *Tales* remain one of Atwood's main sources of inspiration, too (cf., e.g., Wilson 1993; Sullivan 1998; Ljungberg 1999). Although she will later call Tolkien's books "plot-centred otherworld fantasies" (1982:274), Atwood included *The Lord of the Rings* in her research for her (unpublished) Harvard doctoral thesis, entitled *Nature and Power in the English Metaphysical Romance of the Nineteenth and Twentieth Centuries* (*Atwood papers*).[2] Her bibliography contains a number of fantastic works

---

1 The poem is also an ironic dialogue with A.M. Klein's «Portrait of the poet in a landscape» (which, in turn, is a dialogue with James Joyce's *Portrait of the Artist as a Young Man*). Klein was a Montreal poet of the generation before Atwood.

2 Here and henceforth, *Atwood papers* refers to the collection of Atwood's unpublished manuscripts in the Thomas Fisher Library of Rare Books in Toronto.

such as George MacDonald's *Phantastes* and *Lilith*, E. R. Eddison's *The Worm Ouroboros*, Herbert Read's *The Green Child*, C.S. Lewis's *Narnia* books, Rider Haggard's *She* (for which she has written the foreword to the most recent edition), and, as her last example, J.R.R. Tolkien's *The Lord of the Rings*. Her analyses of the various representations of Nature and power point forward to their reappearance in her own fiction which explores these issues and exposes their ideological and constructed character.

But what precisely is the "English metaphysical romance" and how does it apply to Tolkien's novel? Atwood describes it as a romance sub-genre, which is different from Utopian, Gothic or historical fiction; neither is it fairy story nor science fiction, which it sometimes resembles. The genre's main issue is the battle between supernatural good and supernatural evil, a problem central to many literary genres; Atwood's interest centers on how the identity and character of evil and the enemy change over time, thus functioning as indicators of the social and political context in which they were written.[3] Nature and power are the two major nexus of ideas, in which these changes become visible: Nature, as it is represented in various superhuman female figures, and power, as it is portrayed in the guise of diverse superhuman male figures who are either "kings or rulers, or their evil opponents" (*Atwood papers*).

Atwood's preoccupation with the supernatural is in fact a persistent one.[4] As Rosemary Sullivan (1998:176) argues, she seems to have been speculating on the function and nature of the supernatural in several papers already during her time as a student at the University of Toronto; much later, in 1994, she told Sullivan in an interview that "the supernatural is a valued and necessary part of human mentality" (1998:176). What she does

---

3   Atwood mentions George MacDonald's attempt to turn his family into a Scottish clan; the idealistic Socialism of William Morris; Rider Haggard's bitter complaints about the way "they" (the government) were running things, a contempt he shared with C.S. Lewis; J.R.R.Tolkien's dismay with the increasing materialism he saw spreading around him. As Atwood points out, all these writers were convinced that Industrialism was ruining the country, and although not overtly religious, they all opposed the materialistic society (*Atwood papers*).

4   For an in-depth discussion of Nature and ideology in Canadian literature, see Atwood's *Strange Things: The Malevolent North in Canadian Literature* (1995).

not say but which her fiction makes clear is that what she is investigating is female stereotypes, or, rather, how women are portrayed as archetypes in fiction. Atwood's view of Nature is therefore as a cultural and therefore ideological myth. As she has pointed out in her discussion of Nature in her popular critical study, *Survival: A Thematic Guide to Canadian Literature*, landscapes in literature are often "interior landscapes; they are maps of a state of mind" (Atwood 1972:49). Representations of Nature, she suggests, therefore reflect their authors' relationships to the political and social system within which they live: the *manner* in which Nature is represented, and especially, the particular kind of threat that Nature poses – or is herself exposed to – function as indicators of the philosophical ideas current at the time of publication. In the case of the English metaphysical romance, Atwood traces the female superhuman Nature back to Romanticism, where she appears mystical and wise, an "invisible spirit of Wordsworth's benevolent Nature, who can only be fathomed by the poet's intuition" (*Atwood papers*). With the Victorian writers such as Charles Kingsley, George MacDonald and William Morris, this "invisible spirit" was turned into a female deity, semi-deity or supernatural lady and given a central function of the narrative. That changed with the publication of Darwin's *The Origin of Species* in 1859: with the doctrine of the survival of the fittest as a driving force behind the plot, representations of Nature turn cruel and merciless, "Nature red in tooth and claw" (*Atwood papers*): a resilient example is the description of the hazardous journey through the realm of Kôr undertaken by Holly and Leo, narrator and protagonist of Rider Haggard's allegorical romance *She* (1887). Only after the shattering experience of World War I does a benevolent Nature goddess appear: first, in E.R. Eddison's *The Worm Ouroboros* (1922), which was read by the Inklings, and then in *The Lord of the Rings* (1954-55).

In Atwood's discussion of the metaphysical opposition between supernatural good and supernatural evil, she calls attention to the fact that, in Tolkien's world, 'evil' is associated with the cold intellect (as Sauron's eye which Frodo sees in Galadriel's magic mirror), and with the abstract, in the sense of an absence of sensory pleasures. 'Good' has to do with the heart, the senses, the past, the imagination and their creative results, songs and story-telling. These are all abilities ascribed to Elves, Hobbits, Men, Ents, and Dwarves. It is on their side, the 'good' side, that we find the three Nature-goddesses, one immanent (Goldberry), one transcendent (Elbereth Gilthoniel), and one half-way between (Galadriel).[5] As Atwood argues, Goldberry, whom the fellow travelers meet in the house of Tom Bombadil, is a Nature spirit who has no power outside Nature. She is the "River-daughter" who sits with "her feet in wide vessels of green and brown earthenware" (Tolkien 1995:120). She is entirely dependent on Nature for her survival: when Nature is destroyed, so is she. At the other end of the scale Tolkien places Elbereth Gilthoniel, the transcendent Nature-goddess of *The Lord of the Rings*. Elbereth remains mysterious and unknown: Tolkien never gives us much information about her, neither in the text itself, nor in the Appendices, other than that she is called "Varda, Queen of Stars" in the "Blessed Realm." Elbereth, the starry Sky-Queen in the country "beyond the West," who represents the ultimate good, is opposed by Sauron in his dark tower, as the ultimate evil. Like Sauron, who only appears as an eye, Elbereth is never seen in person but remains an other-wordly power whose name is enough to to protect those fighting for the "good" side: the invocation of her name saves Frodo from the Ringwraiths and the Orcs, and lets Sam pass through the "Watchers" in Cirith Ungol, when he uses it for a pass-word in combination with the phial of Galadriel. Both sides use delegates to fight their battles: Saruman fights for the Dark Lord and Mordor, and Galadriel and the forest of Lothlórien for Elbereth and the Far West in Middle-earth.

The most tangible Nature-goddess Tolkien supplies is thus Galadriel, the Lady of Lothlórien. She is the "Mistress of Magic who dwells in the Golden Wood" (Tolkien 1995:652), and it is to her that Elrond sends the group of travelers after Frodo's narrow escape from the Ringwraiths. As Atwood argues, the role of the male ruler of the Elves, Lord Celeborn, is played down: in Lothlórien, it is Galadriel, "the Lady, [whose] 'favour'

---

5   As Atwood points out in her foreword to a recent edition of Haggard's *She* (2002:xxiii), in Tolkien, "She splits into two: Galadriel, powerful but good, who's got exactly the same water-mirror as the one possessed by She; and a very ancient, cave-dwelling man-devouring spider-creature named, tellingly, Shelob."

counts, who wields power and makes decisions and gives advice. She takes a much more active part in the fight against Sauron than do either Goldberry and Elbereth: she was the first summoner of the White Council" (*Atwood papers*). But Galadriel's power is limited and she knows that the days of Lothlórien are counted: if Frodo fails, they will all perish; if he succeeds, her power will still be diminished. That also means that Lothlórien will be restricted to mortal time, ceasing to be the door to time past that Frodo experiences when he enters the magic forest. As Atwood points out, Tolkien posits Lothlórien as "the land of the heart's desire," which has her designate it as the "locus of the nostalgic imagination: to enter it is to become part of a Wordsworthian art, an art of memory, of the past recovered as Paradise" (*Atwood papers*).

Atwood's analyses of the representation of Lothlórien, as an organic Paradise endangered by evil forces, and of the function of these Nature Goddesses point forward to discussions of these issues in her own fiction. When Frodo enters Lothlórien, his sensory perception are heightened: he feels that the colours are "fresh and poignant, as if he had at that moment first perceived them and made for them names new and wonderful." He feels he is a part of Nature: "never before had he been so suddenly and so keenly aware of the feel and texture of a tree's skin and the touch of it (...); it was the delight of the living tree itself" (Tolkien 1995:3441-42). In *Surfacing* (1972/1987), Atwood's second novel, the nameless narrator goes back to her childhood wilderness in her nostalgic search for the past, only to find it threatened by hostile forces, in the form of industry and tourism. "[T]he disease [which] is spreading up from the south" (Atwood 1987:3) is both acid rain and what the narrator thinks are American tourists, who pollute Nature with modern technology. The narrator notes that "they now have seaplanes to hire" (1987:3); the tourists are fishing the lakes empty with their "raygun fishing rods" and "stuff[ing] the pontoons of their seaplanes with illegal fish (Atwood 1987:142). And, as her quest proceeds, she has a vision which proves to be as empowering as Frodo's meeting with Lothlórien and Galadriel, although Atwood gives the visionary experience of *her* narrator a more hallucinatory character, reminiscent of shamanic initiation rites.[6] Dizzy from near starvation, she has a vision of the primeval forest of the Amerindian world of long ago (Atwood 1987:216-17): "The forest leaps upward, enormous, the way it was before they cut it, columns of sunlight frozen; the boulders float, melt, everything is made of water, even the rocks." In her state of heightened awareness, she, too, feels as if she is becoming connected with the earth and the wilderness landscape: "I lean against a tree, I am a tree leaning" (Atwood 1987:217). This experience, in which the narrator feels as if she is merging with Nature, enables her later to 'surface' back into reality and to assert herself in a world in which, until now, she has only seen herself as a powerless victim.

This transformation is, however, generated by a powerful Nature-goddess. She appears as the narrator's dead mother, who enables our protagonist to heal her spiritual wounds. She is one of many Nature-goddesses who crop up in various versions throughout Atwood's fiction. Already in her polemic and influential 1972 study *Survival: A Thematic Guide to Canadian Literature*, she discusses the tendency in literature to make "Woman-Nature metaphors or equations." Her own fiction presents us with a plethora of re-visioned Nature- or Earth-mothers that explore and reflect on these patterns, sometimes in a highly parodic manner. In her first novel, *The Edible Woman*, (1969/1990), for example, in which her narrator-protagonist Marian MacAlpin rebels against social pressures on women by developing an eating disorder, her two friends Ainsley and Clara are both parodic images of the maternal (Nature-goddess) principle, although in different fashions. Clara, who enters the narrative already noticeably pregnant, is the passive Earth-mother who does not question her biological destiny, whereas Ainsley, Marian's roommate, sees motherhood as an ideological project that women must undergo because it "fulfils [their] deepest femininity" (Atwood 1990:41). But in *Surfacing*, a quest narrative which mixes realism and fantasy, the Nature-goddess, in the guise of its protagonist's dead mother, acquires a vital function in the transformation that the 'surfacer' undergoes. The story, whose underlying theme is an

---

6 For a discussion of shamanism in *Surfacing*, see e.g., George Woodcock (1976:85), Marie-François Guédon (1983:91-111), and Kathryn VanSpanckeren (1988:197).

archetypal quest into the wilderness, starts out as a woman's search for a missing father. As the quest proceeds, it is her mysteriously powerful and life-giving mother who becomes the focus of her search. Increasingly, thoughts of her mother occupy her, as she sees the traces her mother has left behind: her garden which keeps on growing, and the blue jays which still keep returning to the cottage. In the narrator's mind, her mother becomes synonymous with wild, natural and nurturing space, as opposed to her father's rationalist view of life; it is this archetypal strength that enables the narrator to surface through patriarchal language and to find a form for her own survival. This forceful and poetic image of a holistic female principle recurs in *Cat's Eye* (1989), dramatically enacted in the painter Elaine Risley, the novel's I-narrator. Elaine's character is contrasted with that of her brother Stephen, a famous astrophysicist, whose reliance on logic and reason ultimately leads to his death at the hands of terrorists. But in this novel, too, Atwood introduces a supernatural Nature-goddess. She appears to Risley as Isis, the regenerating and re-membering avatar of the Great Goddess, who saves Risley's life as a child, when she almost dies from exposure. This mysterious apparition will remain an important source of Risley's creativity in her adult career as a painter. Her pivotal function in the narrative emphasizes how much *Cat's Eye* is a quest narrative, with many fairy-tale attributes: Elaine's return to Toronto to search for lost time has her embark on a journey into a magic world inhabited by typical fairy-tale characters. We will meet "old ghosts, cruel stepsisters, deceitful witches and wizards, disappointing princes, a merciful fairy godmother, and tests to be faced alone in an alien inner landscapes" (Wilson 1993:296).[7] Although both postmodern and ironic, it is the Nature-goddess who, as the "fairy godmother," both initiates and facilitates the rite of passage the quester has to endure and who appears visually on the novel's cover and verbally in various representations in the course of the story.

But there is yet another link between *The Lord of the Rings* and Atwood's *Cat's Eye* and that is the foregrounding of how the magic objects,

---

7 For a discussion of the fairy-tale character of *Cat's Eye* and its fantastic intertexts, see, e.g., Judith McCombs (1992:10) and Sharon Rose Wilson (1993:303-10).

the ring and the cat's eye marble, function in both stories to single out their bearer/protagonist and set them apart from others. These objects also endow them with extraordinary powers to transform themselves and others: the Ring enables Frodo to make himself invisible when he is threatened. In *Cat's Eye*, the cat's eye marble which becomes Risley's talisman allows her "to retreat back into [her] eyes" and to see her tormentors as "shapes ... [and] blocks of color, a red square of a cardigan, a blue triangle of skirt" (Atwood 1989:166). The marble helps her survive the psychological terror she is exposed to by reducing her tormentors into patterns of form and colour, transforming them into "puppets ahead, small and clear" that she can "see [...] or not, at will" (Atwood 1989:166). This ability later develops into a painter's creative vision. But, like the Ring, the magic marble also has it drawbacks: Risley's cat's eye vision alienates her from others and leaves her emotionally numb, reminiscent of how the Ring makes Frodo lonely and suspicious, at times doubting even his faithful Sam.

However, despite the magic realms their characters can escape to and despite their ability to survive their ordeals, both Tolkien's and Atwood's protagonists become maimed for life. Even though Frodo fulfills his quest, he is marked by his wounds and no longer able to settle down to a normal Hobbit life. Atwood's Elaine Risley, too, is forever marked by the near-death incident she experienced as a child, which on the one hand, functions as an archetypal initiation rite to the world of artistic creativity; on the other, her attempts to reconstruct the trauma this incident left her with succeeds only partially. Both questers have been equipped with a shadow, which, as it turns out, is of crucial importance for their respective undertakings. That is also where the two stories take different paths: whereas, in Tolkien, it is thanks to the intervention of Gollum, Frodo's 'shadow', who bites the Ring off Frodo's finger so that it ends up in the fire of Mount Doom, that Frodo's task is finally fulfilled, Atwood's postmodern 'fairy tale' has a less conclusive ending. Although Risley ritually goes back to the scene of the crime, she fails to confront her shadow side, in the character of her old 'friend' who instigated the incident that almost killed her; however, failing to confront her also means the failure of her undertaking to recover the past.

Different as they are, Tolkien and Atwood both exploit images and myths of Nature, at the same time as they endow them with magic and wonder to have them play pivotal parts in their ficional worlds. But, although both locate Nature within the text as the site of dynamic transformation, they have entirely different agendas: whereas, for his part, Tolkien is creating a world around his ancient languages (cf. Shippey 2000), Atwood, while clearly recognizing the romantic appeal of Nature as a cherished myth of origin, also deconstructs and reinvents it by opening it up for a discussion of its contemporary viability. What they have in common, however, is that they are both deeply humanist writers, who concern themselves with fundamental questions of existence, such as the struggle between good and evil and the relationship between Nature and culture. And despite Atwood's 'realistic' and mundane parodies and revisions of the literary canon, which places her characters firmly in a contemporary society,[8] the magic elements in her re-enchantment of Nature provide potential means of transformation that are as archaic as the power of the Ring itself.

CHRISTINA LJUNGBERG holds a PhD from the University of Zurich. She is the author of *To Join, to Fit, and to Make: The Creative Craft of Margaret Atwood* (1999) and has published widely on the interplay between verbal and visual representation in fiction, in particular the use of maps and photographs in fictional texts.

---

8   With three notable exception: *The Handmaid's Tale* (1985) and *Oryx and Crake* (2004), both dystopias set in the future, and *Alias Grace* (1996), which takes place in the first part of the 19th century.

References

ATWOOD, Margaret. 1972. *Survival: A Thematic Guide to Canadian Literature.* Toronto: Anansi.
- - -. 1982. *Second Words: Selected Criticial Prose.* Toronto: Anansi.
- - -. 1987. *Surfacing.* Second edition. First edition 1972. Toronto: Fawcett Crest.
- - -. 1989. *Cat's Eye.* Second edition. First edition 1988. New York: Doubleday.
- - -. 1990. *The Edible Woman.* Second edition. First edition 1969. London: Virago.
- - -. 1995. *Strange Things. The Malevolent North in Canadian Literature.* Oxford: Clarendon.
- - -. Foreword to *She.* 2002. In: HAGGARD, Rider 2002. *She: A History of Adventure.* Toronto: O.W.Toad, v-xxiv.
FRYE, Nothrope. 1971. *The Bush Garden.* Toronto: Anansi.
GUÉDON, Marie-Françoise. 1983. "*Surfacing*: Amerindian Themes and Shamanism." In: GRACE, Sherill E. and Lorna WEIR (eds.) 1983. *Margaret Atwood: Language, Text, and System.* Vancouver: University of British Columbia, 91-111.
HATCH, Ronald B. 2000. "Margaret Atwood, the Land, and Ecology." In: NISCHIK, Reingard (ed.) 2000. *Margaret Atwood: Works and Impact.* Rochester, NY: Camden, 180-2001.
LJUNGBERG, Christina. 1999. *To join, to Fit and to Make. The Creative Craft of Margaret Atwood's Fiction.* Bern and Berlin: Peter Lang.
- - -. 2001. "Iconic Dimensions in Margaret Atwood's Poetry and Prose." In: NÄNNY, Max and Olga FISCHER (eds.) 2001. *The Motivated Sign.* Amsterdam: Benjamins, 351-366.
MCCOMBS, Judith. 1992. "Contrary RE-Memberings: The Creating Self and Feminism in *Cat's Eye*." *Canadian Literature* 129:9-23.
MORTON, W.L. 1972. *The Canadian Identity.* Toronto: University of Toronto.
SHIPPEY, Tom. 2000. *J.R.R. Tolkien, Author of the Century.* London: HarperCollins.
SULLIVAN, Rosemary. 1998. *The Red Shoes: Margaret Atwood Starting Out.* Toronto: Harper*Flamingo*Canada.
TOLKIEN, J.R.R. 1995. *The Lord of the Rings.* One-volume edition. Text of the 2nd revised edition of 1966. First edition 1954-1955 in three volumes. London: HarperCollins.
VANSPANCKEREN, Kathryn. 1988. "Shamanism in the Works of Margaret Atwood." In: VANSPANCKEREN, Kathryn and Jan Garden CASTRO (eds.). 1988. *Margaret Atwood: Visions and Forms.* Carbondale: S. Illinois University Press, 183-204.
WILSON, Sharon Rose. 1993: *Margaret Atwood's Fairy-Tale Sexual Politics.* Toronto: ECW.
WOODCOCK, George. 1976. "Playing Freezing Fire." *Canadian Literature* 70:85.

The Swiss Tolkien Society *EREDAIN*

The Swiss Tolkien Society *EREDAIN* was founded in 1986. Our main aims are to further the study of and the interest in the life and work of late Prof. J.R.R. Tolkien and contribute to the enjoyment of his creation, Middle-earth, in Switzerland.

Our society hosts a monthly discussion group and organises other Tolkien- and fantasy related events such as Middle-earth quizzes, readings, visits to Medieval markets etc. In addition, the society issues a fanzine named *Aglared* once a year. The members of *EREDAIN* share the pleasure in Tolkien's creation with our sister societies in many countries near and far.

If you are interested in our activities, please visit our website at:
> www.eredain.ch

or contact us via:
> kontakt@eredain.ch

or by mail:
> Swiss Tolkien Society
> P.O. Box 1916
> CH-8021 Zurich
> Switzerland

Walking Tree Publishers was founded in 1997 as a forum for publications of material (books, videos, CDs, etc.) related to Tolkien and Middle-earth studies. Manuscripts and project proposals can be submitted to the board of editors (please include an SAE):

Walking Tree Publishers
CH-3052 Zollikofen
Switzerland
e-mail: walkingtree@go.to
http://go.to/walkingtree

Publications:

Cormarë Series
News from the Shire and Beyond. Studies on Tolkien.
    Edited by Peter Buchs and Thomas Honegger. Zurich and Berne 2004. Reprint. 1st edition 1997. (Cormarë Series 1)
Root and Branch. Approaches towards Understanding Tolkien.
    Edited by Thomas Honegger. Zurich and Berne 2005. Reprint. 1st edition 1999. (Cormarë Series 2)
Richard Sturch. *Four Christian Fantasists. A Study of the Fantastic Writings of George MacDonald, Charles Williams, C. S. Lewis and J.R.R. Tolkien.* Zurich and Berne 2001. (Cormarë Series 3)
Tolkien in Translation.
    Edited by Thomas Honegger. Zurich and Berne 2003. (Cormarë Series 4)
Mark T. Hooker. *Tolkien Through Russian Eyes.* Zurich and Berne 2003. (Cormarë Series 5)
Translating Tolkien: Text and Film
    Edited by Thomas Honegger. Zurich and Berne 2004. (Cormarë Series 6)
Christopher Garbowski. *Recovery and Transcendence for the Contemporary Mythmaker: The Spiritual Dimension in the Works of J.R.R. Tolkien.* Zurich and Berne 2004. (Cormarë Series 7). Reprint. 1st edition by Marie Curie Sklodowska University Press, Lublin 2000.
Reconsidering Tolkien
    Edited by Thomas Honegger. Zurich and Berne 2005. (Cormarë Series 8)

Tales of Yore Series
Kay Woollard. *The Terror of Tatty Walk. A Frightener.* CD and Booklet. Zurich and Berne 2000. (Tales of Yore 1)
Kay Woollard, *Wilmot's Very Strange Stone or What came of building "snobbits".* CD and booklet. Zurich and Berne 2001. (Tales of Yore 2)

www.ingramcontent.com/pod-product-compliance
Lightning Source LLC
Chambersburg PA
CBHW050821160426
43192CB00010B/1846